W9-BYN-992

Let's Play Tennis

First published in 1979 by
Octopus Books Limited
59 Grosvenor Street
London W1

© 1979 Octopus Books Limited

ISBN 0 7064 1003 3

Produced by Mandarin Publishers Limited
22a Westlands Road, Quarry Bay, Hong Kong
Printed in Italy - Nuova Grafica Moderna - Verona

Let's Play Tennis

Foreword by Billie Jean King

Robin Davison-Lungley

Editor of Tennis World

Contents

Foreword

You may want to play tennis because you have seen on television or read about the glamorous lives led by the top tennis players of today. And it is true that for the gifted hard-working few tennis can offer an exciting career with lucrative rewards.

But when I had my first tennis lesson in the local park at Long Beach, California, things were very different. Being good at tennis involved considerable time and effort and there was no pot of gold at the end of the rainbow. We took up the game for the challenge of mastering a difficult sport, the spirit of competition, fun, fitness and fresh air. We fought to improve and strove for perfection. But it was the love of the game and the pleasure we got from playing it well that drove us on.

Tennis can be enjoyed on many different levels, from the purely social game at your local park or tennis club to more serious competition like playing for your school, club, or even country. *Let's Play Tennis* is aimed at introducing you to the game of tennis and setting you off on the right foot. Where you go after that is up to you. But whatever your ambitions and whatever your achievements, I only hope you gain as much pleasure from playing tennis as I have done.

Good luck!

Billie Jean King

Introduction

Because you are reading this book, it can be assumed that you are interested in learning how to play tennis. However, you may have picked up *Let's Play Tennis*, keen to discover how the game is played and anxious to get on a tennis court to put what you read into practice. Or you may simply be curious, toying with the idea of taking up tennis, but not fully committed. Either way you will have a better understanding of what is involved in learning how to play tennis by the end of this chapter.

Almost certainly you will already know a little bit about the game of tennis, if only that it is played with rackets and a ball. And you will probably have formed an impression of the sort of game it is—whether it is easy or difficult, safe or dangerous, energetic or relaxing. You will probably have in your mind a picture of the type of people who play tennis and have some knowledge about the places where tennis is played.

Of course, your early impressions may be quite wrong. You may have reached your conclusions with insufficient knowledge of the facts, basing your assessment on too little information. Before starting to learn how to play tennis, or even deciding whether you want to learn how to play, it is worth considering some of the facts and fallacies that surround the game.

First it is not an easy game to play. It looks simple enough when you watch experienced players hitting the ball backwards and forwards on a tennis court, but it is easy to become disillusioned when you try to do the same yourself. The first steps in tennis will be directed towards simply hitting the ball so that it crosses the net and lands in the court on the other side. This sounds fairly simple, particularly if you have watched players like Bjorn Borg and Jimmy Connors thrashing the ball up and down the court at a ferocious pace. But most people's first attempts at hitting a ball with a racket result in a complete miss or, when the ball and racket do make contact, there is no control over the speed and direction of the ball.

Below A tennis instructor explains to a young pupil the correct way to hold a racket. The right technique is particularly important.

Right A young player attempts a difficult overhead stroke.

The player in the picture is concentrating on her opponent as she waits to receive service. The will to win is a great incentive to improvement.

When watching top-class players, it will be common to see the ball going to and fro a dozen times or more. Each player is trying to make it as difficult as possible for his opponent to return the ball. After you have learned how to hit the ball over the net, your next step will be to try to maintain a rally. This involves hitting the ball backwards and forwards with the player on the other side of the net. At first you should try to make it as easy as possible for the person on the other side of the net to return the ball, and he should be doing the same for you. Even so, you will probably have the greatest difficulty in achieving a twelve-stroke rally in your early days of playing the game, so consider the skill of those top-class players.

It is important to arrive quickly at a stage when you can rally the ball with a friend of similar standard as yourself. Walking on to a tennis court for the first time with a new racket and balls is a great novelty, but the novelty will soon wear off when you spend all your playing sessions picking the ball out of the net. Once you can rally a ball, even if it is only for a few strokes, you will have your foot firmly placed on the first rung of the tennis ladder—you will be like a piano pupil who has learned his first tune.

To understand why tennis is such a difficult game, it is necessary to consider the way in which the game is played. Essentially playing tennis involves hitting a ball with an implement, from a variety of positions, in a controlled manner. Tennis would be an easy game if points were scored simply by hitting the ball. But a number of factors make the game rather more complicated. First, you have to hit a ball which is moving. Second, you must hit the ball with a racket. Third, the ball must be hit from a variety of positions—close to your feet, above your head, on your left side or on your right side. And fourth, you have to control the ball when you hit it.

A casual observer may watch a tennis match and not realize that the players on court have developed a variety of methods for hitting the ball across the net—methods based on the way the ball arrives to them and the way they want it to go back to their opponent. These methods are called strokes, and each one requires a technique of its own. A good tennis player must develop several different methods of hitting the ball, unlike most track and field athletes who need know only one technique for pursuing their sport. In this way a tennis player can be compared to a decathlon competitor who uses one technique to pole-vault, a different one for the long jump, another for throwing the discus, and so on.

So, tennis is not an easy game to learn—it is almost certainly more difficult to pick up than other racket-ball games. Why then do we play it? For the answer we must look back over one hundred years to when the game first came into existence. Tennis—or lawn tennis to use the correct name—was invented because people wanted a game that could be played outdoors on the lawns of large houses, and required a certain amount of physical exertion, so the participants could keep fit. There was no other game then in existence that met with all these requirements. Croquet and bowls did not provide much exercise, cricket and golf needed large open areas and real tennis and rackets could only be played indoors.

Tennis has grown in popularity ever since and is now probably the most widely played ball game in the world. The reasons for its popularity today are the same as when the game first started. Admittedly, lawn tennis is now played on many surfaces other than grass, and of course there are many indoor courts around the world. But it is hard to imagine that tennis would be anywhere near as popular as it is today if it could only be played indoors.

Because tennis is a game of skill and the physical element is less important than in many sports, it can be played to a high standard by a variety of people. Visit a park or tennis club and you will see the courts being used by people of every shape and size, young and old, male and female. In tennis technical expertise is far more important than fitness or strength. An old lady who had mastered the technical side of tennis would easily beat an Olympic athlete who had not developed his strokes. That is not to say that fitness is unimportant. When two equally competent players meet on court, provided their tactical knowledge and temperaments are also balanced, the fitter player should win. But don't be put off if you are not very tall or slight in build—there have been many great tennis players who have been small in stature.

The fact that tennis can be mastered by many different types of people and is played all over the world is a great social plus. As a tennis player you should not find too much difficulty finding people with whom to play wherever you go. It is common practice for tennis players to pack their rackets when going on holiday, knowing that they will be able to find a tennis court when they get there and people to play with.

Tennis also contains a strong element of competition. Strictly speaking, hitting a ball up and down a court, simply seeing how long you can keep going on holiday, knowing that they will be able to find for the game, learn how to hit the ball, but go no further. They get their enjoyment merely from hitting the ball over the net—that is sufficient for them. There is nothing wrong with that provided they are satisfied, but without the scoring system, the rules and the element of competition, it is simply not tennis.

Competition is not in itself a bad thing. Provided you can control your competitive spirit and not let it overpower your good sense, it will provide a great deal of enjoyment. A good competitor at tennis will strive to improve his game, but when he is beaten he will acknowledge that his opponent had something that he did not have. He will analyse his opponent's strengths and endeavour to copy them; he will try to understand his own weaknesses, and do something about them. If you only play people you know you can beat, you may build up your ego, but you won't improve your game.

The final chapter is about getting better. Having acquired the basic skills of tennis, you will almost certainly want to put your game to the test against more experienced competitors. You may want to join a club, enter competitions or even play at Wimbledon. But whatever your tennis ambitions, your real gain should be to enjoy the game.

Tennis is a good way of getting out into the sunshine and fresh air, keeping fit and meeting new people. Because it is an international game you will be able to find tennis courts all round the world and people with whom to play.

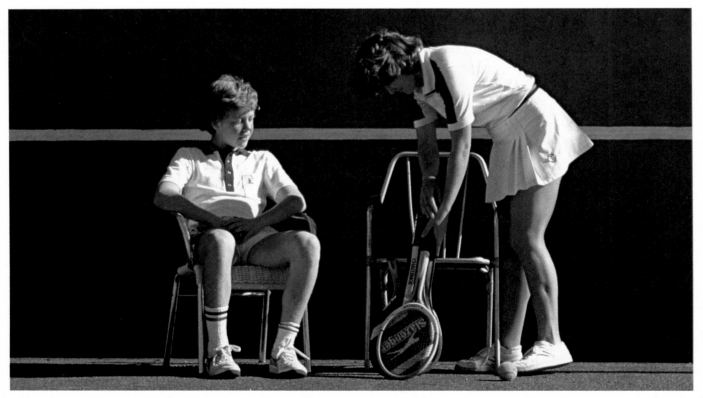

1 The basic strokes

We have already seen that tennis in its most basic form involves two people, one at each end of the court, hitting a ball back and forwards across the net. This activity is called rallying. But in order to keep a rally going for more than a few minutes, the players require a certain amount of technical ability so that they can control the direction and speed of the ball.

Learning how to control the ball is the first step to becoming a good tennis player. Over the years that the game has been played tennis players have developed a range of techniques which enable them to control the ball under the variety of circumstances they come across on the court. These techniques are called strokes and can be divided into three kinds: groundstrokes—for hitting the ball after it has bounced; volleys—for hitting the ball before it has bounced; and overheads—for hitting a ball above the head of the player, as for the service and the smash.

Of course, you can return a tennis ball across the net merely by putting your racket face in the path of the ball and letting the ball bounce off the strings. But the amount of control you would have over the speed and direction of the ball would be very small indeed. To exercise any *real* control over a ball, you have to *hit* it, which means moving your racket to meet the on-coming ball—playing a stroke.

Basically there are three types of movement we make when playing a stroke in tennis: the swing—which we use for hitting our groundstrokes; the punch—which we use for hitting our volleys; and the throw—which we use for hitting overheads.

When you start playing, you will find it very difficult to develop a swing. Golfers spend hours perfecting their swings, but few people realize that a good swing is as important for a tennis player as for a golfer. Of course a golfer has a much easier task than a tennis player—he doesn't have to hit a moving ball. It is for this reason that many beginners shy away from swinging their rackets. After all, with the ball moving and the racket moving it takes considerable skill to make sure that the two meet.

One of the things you will develop as you play tennis is anticipation. To be a good player you will have to be able to 'read' the ball. In other words you will have to know what a ball is going to do—where and how it will bounce—well in advance of making your stroke. When you begin you will just have to be brave, follow the instructions in this book and not worry about the fact that you are a beginner. Every good player had to begin at sometime and even the best player mishits a few balls from time to time.

The three basic movements used by a tennis player when hitting the ball across the net are the swing, the throw and the punch. The swing is the movement used for hitting the ball after it has bounced. The throw is the movement used by a tennis player for hitting overheads. The punch is the movement used for hitting the volley. The diagram below illustrates the movement of the racket when hitting a volley.

The swing (above) is the racket movement used for hitting groundstrokes after the ball has bounced.

The diagram below illustrates the movement of the racket when a player is hitting the ball over his head. The movement is called a throw because it involves the same body action as for throwing a ball or stick.

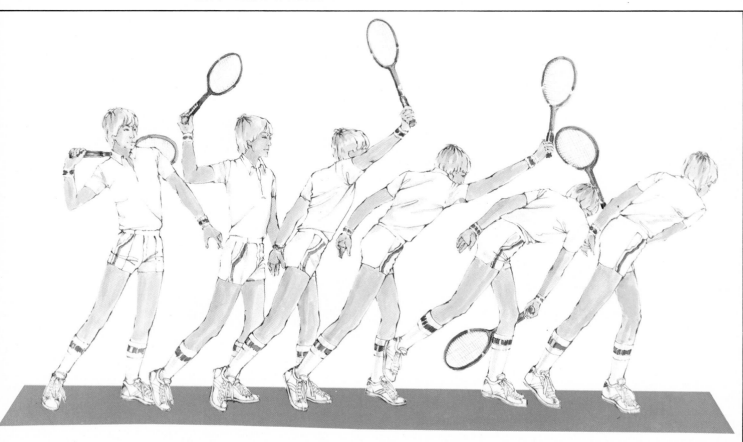

Hitting the ball

Almost as important as the actual stroke itself is hitting the ball with the right part of the racket. The right part of the racket is the strings—in particular the very centre of the strings which we call the sweet spot. This is the area in the face of the racket that has the most elasticity and will give the player the greatest amount of control over the ball.

Hitting the ball 'off centre' will cause the racket to twist in the player's hand, leading to loss of control and, if the ball is mishit regularly, could lead to a blistered hand or arm injury. Tennis players ensure that they always hit the ball in the sweet spot by watching the ball right on to the centre of the strings.

When playing tennis, it is a great temptation to look away from the ball a moment or two before you hit it. You feel that by looking in the direction you want the ball to travel, you can somehow will it to go there.

Unfortunately, tennis balls are more responsive to the sweet spot than they are to will power, so the hit-and-hope method should be avoided.

Practise watching the ball by getting a box of balls and numbering them from one to six. The numbers should be large and clear. Ask a friend to stand at the far side of the net and hit or throw the balls to you. You have to hit the balls back to your friend, calling out the number on the ball as you strike it.

When hitting a groundstroke, it is important not only to hit the ball in the sweet spot, but to hit it at the right height after it has bounced. The right height to hit a groundstroke is when the ball is between knee- and waist-high. As a rule the ball will have reached

When playing ground-strokes, the ideal place to hit the ball is when it is between knee- and waist-height of your body. This will allow you the best swing trajectory. The ball should be falling after reaching the full height of its first bounce and be slightly in front of your leading foot.

the top of its bounce and be on its way down for the second bounce. A few of the world's top players hit the ball before it has reached the top of the bounce, thus giving themselves a split-second's advantage over their opponent. This practice is called 'taking an early ball', or 'hitting the ball on the rise', but it requires considerable skill and should not be attempted by a beginner.

You will soon discover that the height a ball bounces can vary considerably according to the surface of the court—whether hard or soft—the condition of the ball, the way it has been hit to you, and even the weather. If you find the ball is bouncing chest- or even head-high, simply stand back a little further to allow the ball to drop to a comfortable height for you to play your stroke.

So far I have covered the action of the eyes—watching the ball—and the action of the racket arm—swinging, throwing and punching. But playing tennis well involves the use of the whole body. You need your legs to carry you to the ball and your feet to make sure you are in the best position and well balanced when hitting the ball. Your knees should always be bent when playing a groundstroke or volley, and the movement of your shoulders and hips give power to your strokes.

Finally, before covering the individual strokes in detail, it is important that you should know what to do when you are not actually playing a stroke. If you have hit the ball over the net and are waiting for it to be returned to you, or you are simply waiting for the ball to be put in play, you should stand in a position of readiness, sometimes called the ready position.

When you are waiting to receive the ball during a game of tennis, always adopt the position of readiness. This is the stance that will best enable you to move into any shot you will be required to play. When in a ready position, your feet should be comfortably apart with the weight of your body on the balls of your feet. Your knees should be slightly bent and your back gently arched.

Below The right place to hit the ball is in the centre of the strings—the sweet spot.

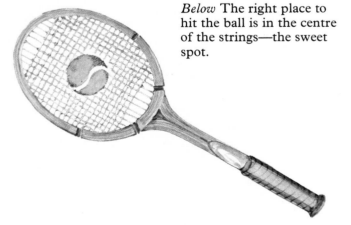

Standing square to the net, your feet should be about shoulder-width apart, with your heels just off the ground and your weight on the balls of your soles. Your knees should be slightly bent and your back should be gently arched. Your racket should be firmly gripped, held with the racket head chest-high diagonally across your body and supported lightly at the throat by your other hand. From this position you will be best placed to move into your next stroke. But remember, once you have played the ball, return to your position of readiness.

The forehand drive

Most people have greater control with either their left or right hand. They find it easier to write, catch a ball or dial a telephone number with one hand or the other. A few people are ambidextrous, that is to say are equally competent with both hands. When describing the individual strokes, I have assumed that the reader is right-handed and will therefore hold his racket in his right hand. If you are left-handed, simply substitute left for right, and vice versa, in my explanations and imagine a mirror-image of the diagrams and photographs. By the way, if you are left-handed, you will be pleased to know that you will be at no disadvantage on the tennis court. Many of the world's best players are 'lefties'.

The forehand strokes are the ones we hit on the right-hand side of our bodies, be they groundstrokes, overheads or volleys. The forehand drive is the groundstroke we use to hit a ball on our right-hand side—that is to say, after the ball has bounced once. For tactical reasons that will become clear later, this stroke is usually hit by a player at the back of the court and is directed towards the baseline at the opposite end of the court.

First make sure you are holding the racket properly. Over the years a number of different ways have developed for holding the racket when hitting tennis strokes. In this book you will find explanations of three grips: the eastern forehand (for hitting forehand drives); the eastern backhand (for hitting backhand drives); and the continental (for hitting overheads and volleys). Having mastered these methods of holding the racket you need never bother with any other grip.

An illustration of the eastern forehand grip appears above as well as a simple method of making sure

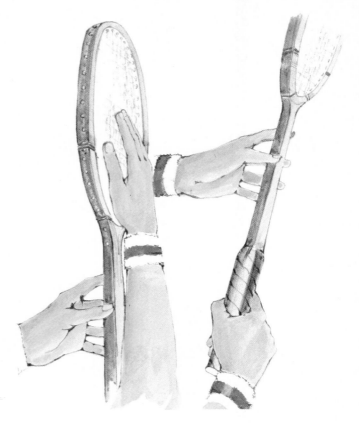

The eastern grip: place the right hand flat against the strings. Run it down the handle until the base of the palm meets the butt of the racket handle.

that you are holding the racket correctly. Always check that you have got the right grip before attempting your stroke.

The drives, both forehand and backhand, are 'swinging' strokes. In both cases the racket is taken well back and swung at the ball. After making contact with the ball, the racket head continues its swing, ending up high in front of the player. The process of taking the racket back is called the backswing; the

The forehand drive: the player holds the racket, supporting the throat with his left hand.

As the ball bounces he steps across with his left foot so that he is sideways to the net.

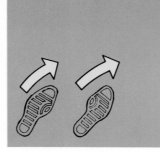

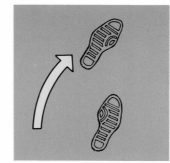

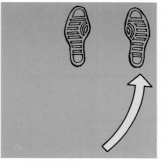

| For the forehand drive start in a ready position with feet apart. | As you see the ball approaching, swivel your toes to the right. | Step diagonally across with your left foot so that your body is sideways to the net. | After striking the ball, move your right foot alongside your left. |

movement of the racket after it has struck the ball is called the follow-through.

When you are next on a tennis court, try this method of hitting a forehand drive. Stand towards the back of the court, square to the net in your ready position. But instead of supporting the racket with your left hand, hold a ball. Toss the ball so that it lands about a metre (1 yd) in front of you and in line with the outside edge of your right foot. At the same time take your racket back so that your extended arm is level with your right shoulder, pointing towards the back of the court and with the racket head directed to the sky. As the ball reaches the full height of its bounce, step diagonally across with your left foot in the direction of the bouncing ball, swinging your racket in a shallow arc aimed at hitting the ball between knee- and waist-high. Allow the racket to swing through after it has contacted the ball, finishing high in front of you, with your arm extended in the direction of the far end of the court and the racket head pointing towards the sky.

These are the basic actions of the forehand drive. If you have followed them correctly, you will have found that as you swung the racket towards the ball, you transferred the weight of your body from the

back foot to the front foot. Then, as the racket followed through after hitting the ball, your right foot swung round to a position alongside the left.

Repeat this exercise as often as possible so that you get used to the movements of the forehand drive. When you feel that the stroke is instinctive and that you are hitting the ball consistently across the net using this method, try and apply the same technique to hitting a ball that is coming towards you. Get a friend to stand about 10 or 15 m (10–15 yd) away and throw the ball towards you on your forehand side. Then try the same exercise with your friend hitting the balls to you from across the net.

If you have the correct grip and have mastered the swing, the only problem you may find is getting into the right position to hit the ball. Unfortunately there is no magic formula for this. Some people can position themselves instinctively. We call these people natural ball players and say they have ball-sense, but for most of us the ability to get in the best place to play the ball comes with practice and experience.

Remember, to hit a good forehand drive you must step into the ball when making the stroke, so try to judge where the ball is going to land and stand well back.

| The player swings his racket in a gentle arc | aiming to meet the ball level with his right foot. | The player continues to swing the racket so that it | finishes head-high, his racket arm fully extended. |

The backhand drive

We now know how to cope with a ball that bounces on the right-hand side of the body, but what if the ball is directed to the other side? The thought of hitting the ball on the 'wrong' side of the body fills many beginners with terror, but with a little practice and the right technique you will be able to return a ball from your left-hand side as easily as one from the right.

The right technique for hitting a ball that bounces on the wrong side of your body is the backhand drive.

Like its forehand cousin, the backhand stroke is a swinging action. And many of the rules we have learned for our forehand drive can be applied to the backhand drive. Take the racket well back, turn sideways to the net by stepping at an angle with the right foot, the wrist being firm and the knees bent when you hit the ball, and then complete the follow-through with the racket high in the air in front of the body. Even the position of the ball in relation to your body is the same for the backhand drive as it was for the forehand—between knee- and waist-high and level with the front of your leading foot.

But there are several basic differences between the backhand and forehand drive, and these must be mastered if a player is to develop the stroke successfully.

Most beginners make the mistake of trying to hit a backhand with a forehand grip. The eastern forehand grip is the best way of holding the racket when hitting a ball on the right-hand side of the body, mainly because the wrist is behind the line of the ball—you are, in effect, 'pushing' the ball over the net. With this

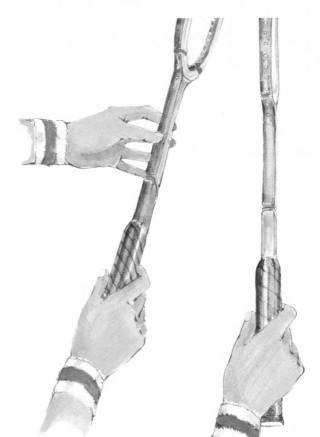

The eastern backhand grip: start with an eastern forehand grip and rotate the hand a quarter of a turn. Extra control can be obtained by running the thumb diagonally along the flat of the racket grip.

grip you can keep a firm wrist on impact with the ball. But hitting a ball on the left of the body with an eastern forehand grip is rarely successful. The wrist is in front of the ball on impact and will tend to 'wobble', causing loss of control.

By rotating your hand anti-clockwise for about a

The backhand drive: the the player is standing square to the net with the racket held diagonally.

As the ball approaches, the player changes his grip, stepping diagonally across with his right foot.

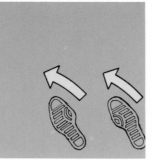

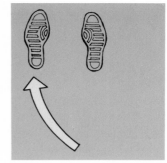

For the backhand drive start in a ready position, feet square to the net.

As the ball approaches on the left-hand side, swivel on your toes to the left.

Step diagonally across with your right foot, turning sideways to the net.

After striking the ball, bring your left foot alongside the right.

quarter of a turn on the racket handle from the eastern forehand grip, you will find that you can hit a ball on the left-hand side of your body with the wrist slightly behind the line of the ball, thus reducing the chance of any wrist-wobble on impact. In fact, the backhand grip is still considerably weaker than the forehand grip, which means that there is far less margin for error when hitting the backhand drive.

Standing in a position of readiness, but holding the racket in the right hand in the eastern backhand grip, and a ball in the left hand, toss the ball about a metre (1 yd) in front of you and in line with the outside edge of your left foot. At the same time take your racket back so that your arm is stretched across your chest and the head of the racket is behind your left shoulder. As you take the racket back, swivel on the balls of your feet so that your toes are pointing towards the left-hand side of the court. Your shoulders and hips should now be sideways to the net. With your right foot step diagonally across in the direction of the bouncing ball and swing the racket head in a gentle loop aimed at meeting the ball after it has reached the full height of its bounce. The racket should be allowed to continue its swing after striking the ball, finishing high in the air in front of you. As you follow through with the racket, your left foot should swing forward, ending alongside the right one, and from here returning to a ready position is a simple adjustment.

Repeat this exercise until the movements are 'grooved' and then get a friend to 'feed' your back-hand, first throwing the ball from your side of the net and then hitting balls to your backhand side. Remember that you will usually be hitting the drives from the back of the court. Aim high over the net— between 1·2 m and 1·8 m (4–6 ft)—and try to get the ball to bounce within a metre or two (1–2 yd) of the far baseline. Remember too that the ball should be struck between knee- and waist-height and just in front of the right foot. Hitting the ball too late will send it off to the left of the court; too early, and the ball will veer away to the right. Because your grip for the backhand is weaker, hitting the ball in the centre of the strings and at the right place in relation to the body, is of the utmost importance.

The player makes contact with the ball between knee- and waist-height in front of his right foot.

The follow-through for the backhand drive is high into the air. The player's arm is fully extended.

The two-handed backhand drive

Many players feel that they do not have time to change their grip, or that even with an eastern backhand their wrist is not strong enough to control the ball on the left-hand side of the body. This is particularly true of very young players—between the ages of four and ten years old. These people often prefer to hold the racket with two hands when hitting a backhand drive.

Although the double-handed grip is much stronger than the one-handed variety, reducing wrist-wobble and allowing a greater margin for error, holding the racket with two hands restricts the player's reach and upsets his balance. However, many top players prefer this stroke, so it is worth experimenting with if you have difficulty with a one-handed backhand.

Use a double eastern grip to hit a two-handed backhand. Start with the racket held in the right hand with an eastern forehand grip. Place the palm of the left hand in the centre of the strings with the fingers pointing towards the racket's tip. Now, keeping the hand flat, run it down along the handle of the racket until the base of the palm touches the thumb of the right hand. Grasp the handle firmly.

When hitting the backhand with a two-handed grip, shorten the swing. Take the racket back so that the head is shoulder-high—your hands will be about level with the top of your abdomen. Step towards the ball as you would with the one-handed stroke. On impact both arms will be bent at the elbows. Follow through with the racket head to about shoulder-height.

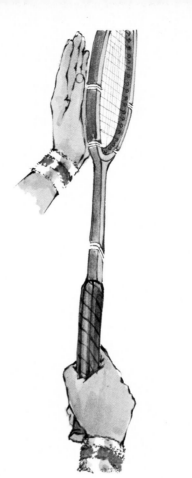

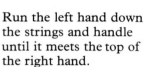

Above The two-handed backhand grip: hold the racket in the right hand in an eastern forehand grip.

Below Note that the swing and follow-through are shorter for a double-handed backhand.

Run the left hand down the strings and handle until it meets the top of the right hand.

Right A young player practises a double-handed backhand with a coach.

A simple service

When you have developed a degree of consistency in your groundstrokes, you will, no doubt, wish to start an actual game of tennis. The rules and scoring system are covered in the next chapter, but before you start playing games you will have to learn how to serve.

The service is the method by which the ball is put into play at the start of each point. The player stands behind the baseline and hits the ball across the net so that it bounces in the area which is called the service box.

We have seen how the forehand and backhand drives are 'swinging' movements; the service is a 'throwing' movement. When making an overhead service, or delivery, as it is sometimes called, the player uses the same body actions as he would to throw a ball or a stick across the net.

Practise the service action by standing behind the baseline, sideways to the net. Hold the racket in your right hand with the neck of the racket balanced on your right shoulder. Pretend that you are trying to throw the racket as far over the net as possible, but keep a firm grip on the handle. You will probably find that the head of the racket has finished down alongside your left calf, and that in order to stop yourself from falling forward, your right leg has swung round into the court. This is the basic throwing action you will use for your overhead service.

Now try using the same movement to hit a ball over the net. Still standing sideways and with a ball in your left hand, balance the racket as before on your right

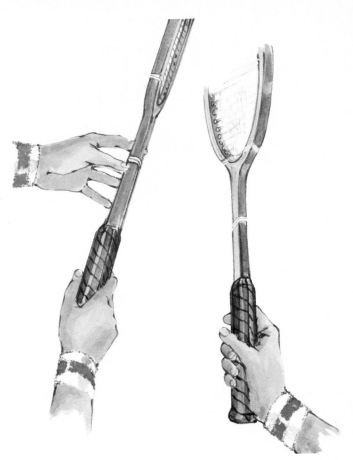

The continental grip: hold the racket as if it were an axe and you were going to chop firewood.

From the eastern forehand grip rotate your hand an eighth of a turn clockwise.

shoulder. With your left hand toss the ball up in front of you to a height about 1·2–1·5 m (4–5 ft) above your head. Now, using the same throwing action, try to hit the ball with the strings of the racket.

A simple service: the racket head starts behind the server's back, his right arm bent.

The server is sideways to the net, his feet apart.

With his left hand he throws the ball up.

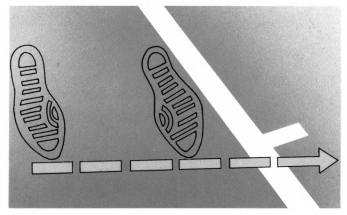

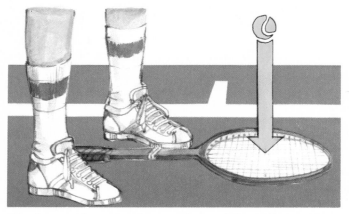

The feet should be behind the line when serving and comfortably apart.

The line shown is the direction in which the service should travel.

Check your throw-up by placing a racket on the ground at your feet as

shown. The ball should land on the strings of your racket.

With practice you should be able to reach a high standard of consistency using this method. But a few minor adjustments will greatly improve your technique.

The best grip for the service is the continental grip. Holding the racket in an eastern forehand grip, simply rotate the hand anti-clockwise an eighth of a turn. The continental grip is sometimes called the chopper grip, because you hold the racket in the same way as you would hold an axe when chopping logs for the fire.

When serving, your feet should be comfortably apart and behind the baseline. If you were to draw an imaginary line from the toe of your back foot to the toe of your front foot and continue the line into the court, this is the direction the ball should travel when you serve.

Throwing the ball up in exactly the right place is one of the secrets of a good service. The action of the

left hand is as important as that of the right, when developing a good overhead delivery. The ball should be hit with the racket arm fully extended over the server's head so it is important to throw the ball nice and high. If the throw-up is too far forward, the ball will end up in the net; if it is too far back, it will sail out of the end of the court. The correct place to throw the ball up is a little way in front of you. If, instead of hitting the ball when it is in the air, you allow it to drop to the ground, the ball should land 10–20 cm (4–8 in) in front of your leading foot.

The method of delivery just described is a simplified version of the service used by the top professional players. Once you have mastered the basic movements described in this section, you should try to develop a service rhythm—this will improve the accuracy, consistency and power of your deliveries. The way to improve your service by developing a rhythm is described in Chapter 4.

At point of impact the server's arm is fully

extended.

The racket follows through across the server's body

finishing down alongside his left calf.

2 The rules of the game

The court

Now that you have learned a few of the simple methods of hitting the ball across the net, you will probably want to start playing a game, rather than just hitting the ball to and fro. But before you can play a game of tennis, you will have to know the rules and the right way to score. A book of rules can be bought from your national tennis association at a small cost, and everyone who intends taking the game seriously should get a copy.

The rules of tennis not only lay down what you can and cannot do on a tennis court, and tell you how to score, they also give exact details about the measurement of a tennis court and the net. That way you can play tennis in any country in the world and know that the courts are exactly the same size and shape as the ones on which you learned how to play.

Unless you actually plan to make your own court, its exact measurements will not be of great importance to you, although you should be familiar with the names of the various parts. Basically, a tennis court is a flat rectangular area with a net across the centre of

Below The dimensions of a tennis court marked out for singles and for doubles play.

Right The height of the net can be checked by holding one racket on top of another.

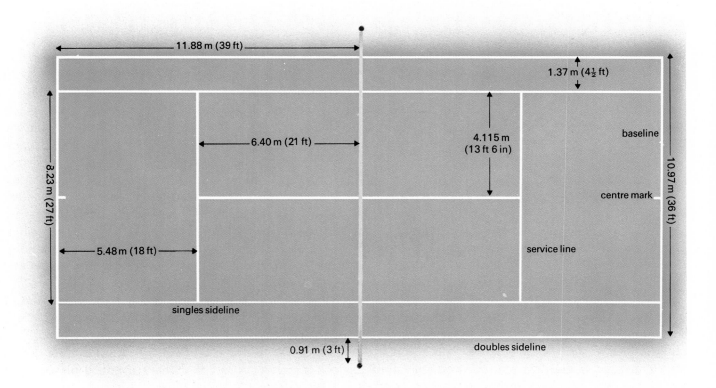

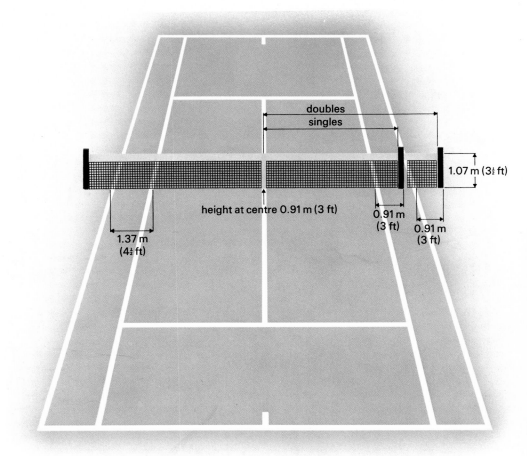

doubles
singles

height at centre 0.91 m (3 ft)

0.91 m (3 ft)

0.91 m (3 ft)

1.07 m (3½ ft)

1.37 m (4½ ft)

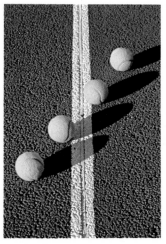

Left It should be noted that a tennis net is a different height at the net posts and the centre. The centre strap should be taut during play.

Below The rules state that if a ball touches a line it is considered to be in the area bounded by the line. This photograph of the right-hand sideline shows four balls. Only the ball on the far right is out.

the narrow part. The net is supported on each side by upright posts called net posts located just outside the playing area. The short sides of the rectangle are called the baselines and the long sides are the sidelines.

On each side, and 6·4 m (21 ft) away from the net, a line is drawn across from one sideline to the other, running parallel with the net. This is called the service line. Another line is drawn from the centre of the service line on one side of the net to the centre of the service line on the other side. This is called the centre line and divides the area on each side of the net into four boxes which are called the service boxes. At the centre of each baseline is a short line 10 cm (4 in) long running into the court, and known as the centre mark.

This is all quite simple really, except for one little complication. The rules stipulate that the game of doubles should be played on a wider court. In fact, most tennis courts you will ever encounter are drawn up for doubles as well as singles play. An extra side-line is added 1·37 m (4½ ft) beyond the singles side-line, to each side of the court, and the baselines are extended to reach these new lines. When playing singles, the outside lines should be ignored, but in doubles they represent the outside of the court.

Although the measurements of the court do not really concern you, what the rule book has to say about the net is another matter. You may find in some cases that you have to put up the net yourself, or when the net has already been fixed, you will almost certainly have to check that it is at the correct height.

The rule book stipulates that the net should be 1·07 m (3½ ft) high at the net posts and 0·91 m (3 ft) high in the centre. It also specifies that the net should be held taut by a band passing over the top of the net at its centre point and attached to a fitting on the court. In other words—it should not just droop. In fact, this is a rather pedantic rule, and you will find that many of the courts on which you play don't even have centre bands. Even so, it is important to check the height of the net at its centre before starting a game. If you don't have a tape measure (some courts have their own measuring sticks attached to the net posts), you will be able to measure the net with two rackets. By standing one racket upright on the ground beside the centre of the net, then resting the head of a second racket on top of the first, you can find the correct height of the net. However, before you set out for a game of tennis, it is worth checking the exact measurements of your racket. Although most adult rackets are the same size, junior rackets are usually a little smaller. You can also buy rackets with very small handles designed for players between the ages of three and five years.

One of the strange things about the rule book of tennis is that it covers in great detail the size and shape of a tennis court—even the width of the lines. The dimensions of the ball are also given in minute detail, but nothing in the rule book prevents a player from using a racket of any size, shape or material he chooses. You could quite legitimately win a tennis match using a frying pan if you so choose.

Starting and scoring

When starting to play tennis, many people find the method of scoring a little confusing at first. In fact, it is the use of the numbers which makes the system appear more complicated than it really is. In a match you will be dealing in points, games and sets—almost like a currency.

A tennis match is won by the person (or pair in doubles) who wins the most sets. A match can be the best of three sets or the best of five. In the first instance the person who wins two sets first is the winner and in the second, the person who wins three sets first.

A set is a series of games. The player who wins six games is the winner of the set, provided he has a two-

Deciding who serves first can be done by one player spinning his racket while the other player calls 'rough' or 'smooth'.

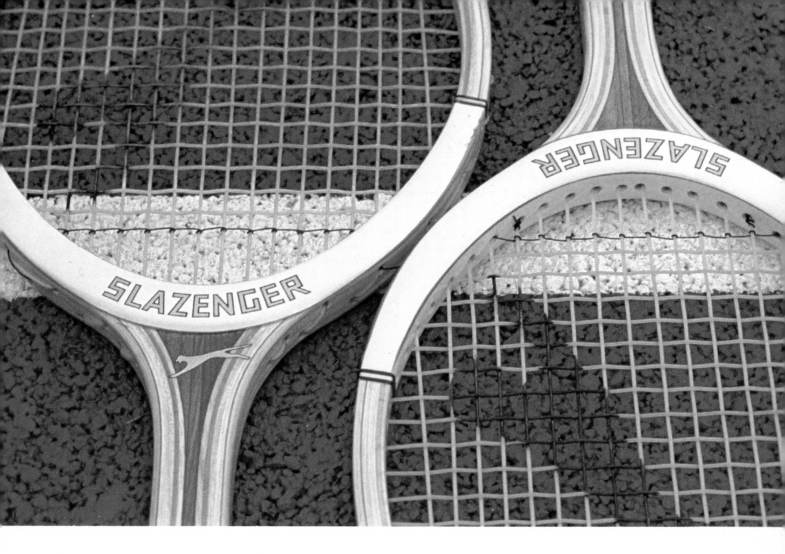

game lead over his opponent. If by the time he reaches six games he only has a one-game advantage, the set continues until one or other player takes a two-game lead.

A game is made up of a series of points. The player who wins the first point in a game is awarded 15 points. In tennis the server's score is always given first, so if the server wins the first point, the score is 15–love (love means nil). If the receiver wins the first point, the score is love–15. If the person who lost the first point wins the second point, the score is 15–all. The second point a player wins brings his score to 30, the third point brings it to 40, and the fourth point gives him the game. However, if both players reach 40 points, it is called deuce and one player must win two consecutive points before winning the game. The player who wins the first point after deuce is said to have the advantage.

A point begins when one of the players serves the ball. If the service is a fault, the server has a second chance. If the second service is a fault then the receiver wins the point. If, however, the service is 'good', that is to say conforming with all the rules governing the service, then it is up to the receiver to make a 'good' return. A 'good' return involves hitting the ball with the racket (once only), back over the net, before it has bounced twice. The return, if allowed to bounce, should land in court, although, once the service return has been struck either player is allowed to play the ball before it bounces.

The call of 'rough' or 'smooth' refers to the trebling on the strings.

The racket on the left is smooth; that on the right is rough.

These are the basic rules of the game as they affect the scoring. But the rule book has been drawn up to deal with all eventualities, and some of the more unusual things that might happen on court are covered in more detail at the end of the chapter.

You should now know enough about the scoring system and the rules to be able to play a match, although you may not actually know how to start. Before you begin a match, you will have to decide who is going to serve first. The rules state that this should be decided by a toss. Most tennis players spin a racket to see who will serve first. Almost all tennis rackets have a fine piece of red nylon laced between the upright strings near the throat of the racket. Its purpose is to stop the strings from moving across and it is called trebling. Trebling is laced around the strings in such a way that if you run your finger along the trebling on one surface of the racket, it will feel smooth, but if you turn the racket over and feel the trebling on the reverse face of the racket, it will feel rough. So, one player spins the racket and the other calls rough or smooth. The player who wins the toss can choose to serve (in which case his opponent has choice of ends), or he can choose to receive (in which case his opponent still has choice of ends). He can instead pick the end he prefers (in which case his opponent can choose to serve or receive first).

The service

The player who serves first continues serving throughout the game. His opponent serves in the second game and the service then alternates with each game throughout the match. In doubles, as with singles, one player serves throughout the whole game. After the first game one of the opposing pair serves for a whole game, the partner of the first server serves throughout the third game and the partner of the second server throughout the fourth game. This order of rotation continues until the end of a set. At this point the partners can change the order in which they serve if they so choose.

Having decided who is to serve first, the players take up their positions on each side of the net. The player who is to serve stands anywhere behind the baseline between the centre mark and the sideline to his right. From this position he must throw the ball into the air and hit it with his racket so that it crosses the net and bounces in the service box to his left. If the service is a fault, the server has a second chance. If, however, the ball hits the net before bouncing into the service box, it is called a let and the service is taken again.

A service is a fault if it does not bounce in the correct service box, or if the ball bounces before crossing the

Above A foot-fault.

Below Three types of service: on the left a fault; in the centre a 'good' service; on the right a let.

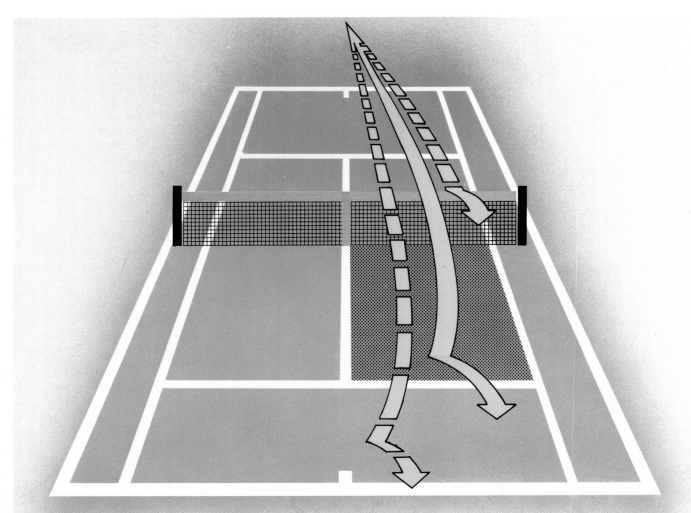

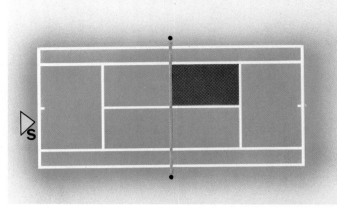

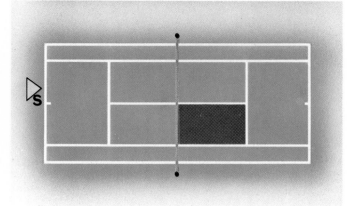

The first service in a game is hit by the server standing to the right of the centre mark and to the left of the sideline into the service box indicated.

The second service in the game is hit by the server standing to the left of the centre mark and the right of the sideline into the service box indicated.

net. It is also a fault when the server starts with his feet in the wrong place or moves them in such a way that he contravenes the foot-fault rule. Ignoring this rule when you are starting to play can lead to bad habits which will be hard to break in later years.

Apart from having your feet in the correct position when you start your service action—behind the base-line and between the centre mark and sideline (or rather an imaginary extension of these lines)—you are not allowed to walk, run or touch the ground with either foot outside the designated service area. You *are* allowed to lift one foot off the ground, provided that your racket strikes the ball before the foot touches down out of bounds, or, if you like, you can jump with both feet while you serve—many top-class players do just this. Remember, being behind the line means just that. If you touch a line—even one of the

imaginary ones—during your service, the service is a fault.

Once the first point has been decided, the server stands behind the baseline between the centre mark and the sideline to his left. He must then attempt to hit the ball across the net into the service box on the right-hand side of the court. The server continues to alternate his service from right to left and left to right throughout the course of the game. Each game is started by the server standing to the right of the centre mark (as he looks down to his opponent's end of the court) and the first ball is always served to the service box across the net and to the left of the server.

Below The back of the player's foot has crossed the centre mark—this is a foot-fault.

Right Another foot-fault. The player's right foot has touched down inside the court.

The ball in play

We now know what constitutes a 'good' service. The server must stand in a given area behind the baseline. We have also briefly covered what constitutes a 'good' return. The ball must be hit with the racket back across the net before it has bounced twice and should land in court. However, the rules take into consideration various unlikely occurrences. For example, what happens if the ball hits a player? In this event, even if he is standing outside the court, the player who has been struck loses the point. A player also loses the point if he touches the net at any time that the ball is in play, or if he leans across and hits the ball before it has crossed to his side of the net. However, when the ball is hit across the net, and having bounced then spins or is blown back across the net, the player is allowed to lean over the net and hit the ball before it bounces on his opponent's side. If it bounces on his opponent's side before he hits it, he loses the point.

There is one occasion when it is not necessary to return the ball *over* the net in tennis. When your opponent's service or return has forced you to run wide to reach the ball, you may be in a position to hit the ball into his court, round the side of the net post. Such a return is quite legitimate, and the ball need not be returned above net-height when being played in this manner.

In the event that a player has left a ball lying in his half of the court, a dangerous thing to do in any case, it is possible for his opponent's return, or service, to hit the loose ball. When this happens, it is almost impossible for the player whose turn it is to play the ball to make a return. However, if he can return it, his shot is 'good'. When a ball is out of reach and a player throws his racket and it hits the ball, he loses the point, whether or not the ball goes back across the net.

It is also a 'good' return when the ball hits the net, or the net post, and bounces into court. But if the ball hits anything else that might be around the court—an umpire's chair for example—it is a fault. It is also a 'good' return if the ball touches one of the boundary lines of the court. Similarly, a service is 'good' if the ball bounces on any of the boundary lines of the service box. A ball that touches a line is considered to be inside the area that the line bounds.

Below If, from this position, the player returns the ball past the outside of the net post so that it lands in court, the return is good. Loose balls should not be allowed to remain on court during play. It is easy for a player to slip.

Right A player must not hit the ball until it has passed to his side of the net. The racket may follow through over the net, but it is a fault if the racket or any part of the player's clothing touches the net.

3 Tactics and training

The purpose of tactics

Learning how to control a ball with your racket is an important step towards becoming a good tennis player. However, like most competitive activities, tennis has another side—the thinking part. You may be able to hit the ball perfectly and make it go anywhere you choose, but unless you use your head as well as your

A player should not come to the net behind a weak shot. Here the player has hit a poor approach shot and advanced to the net. The player on the baseline has hit the ball past her.

Besides being able to hit accurate groundstrokes from the back of the court and angled volleys from the net, a player should develop a drop shot. When the opponent is back at the baseline, he will be able to play a drop shot as shown here.

racket, you will find yourself being beaten by players with much less skill, but with a greater understanding of tennis tactics than yourself.

You may wonder what tactics have to do with sport. That sort of thing is all right on the battlefield, but hardly of use on a tennis court. Surely, tennis is simply a matter of hitting the ball back to the opponent as fast as possible so that he is unable to return it? This attitude is fine until you meet someone who likes people to hit the ball at him as hard as possible, for this enables him to hit it back even harder. So it will not be long before you discover that tactics are as essential to a tennis player as they are to a commander on the battlefield.

The most basic tactic in tennis is to hit the ball out of your opponent's reach. It is far better to hit a soft shot to a part of the court your opponent cannot reach, than to hit a hard ball straight to him. However, this is easier said than done. After all, a tennis court is a relatively small area, and anyone who is at all fit should be able to reach any part of the court in a second or two. Therefore, it is worth considering the ways in which you can hit the ball out of your opponent's range.

When your opponent comes up close to the net, you have two alternatives. Either you can hit the ball high over his head so that it lands near the back of the court—this is called a lob—or you can try and hit the ball round the side of him (often the more difficult alternative). Hitting the ball past a player who has advanced to the net is called a passing shot. The opposite of the lob is the drop shot. This should only be played when your opponent is at the back of the

A player standing at the net is best placed to hit a winner off his opponent's return. At the net the player can angle his volley into any part of the court. Playing the ball at a height above the net allows him to hit down on the ball.

court. The shot consists of gently dropping the ball over the net to land about a metre (3 ft) into your opponent's court. The bounce should be small, making it impossible for the person you are playing to reach.

Besides the lob, passing shot and drop shot, the other main tactics for playing the ball out of reach are the angled groundstroke and the angled volley. It is not at all easy to angle a groundstroke so that it is completely out of range of your opponent. This is because most groundstrokes are hit from the back section of the court where a player is greatly restricted in his range of angles if he wants his return to land in court. However, a player who is standing at the net, hitting the ball before it has bounced, has virtually the whole of his opponent's court in which to angle his return. From such a position it is a simple matter to place the ball out of the opponent's reach. Hitting the ball before it has bounced is called volleying, and because it is so easy to place a volley out of your opponent's reach, getting into a good volleying position is one of the key tactics in tennis.

When playing an opponent who is the same standard, or better than you, you will find that you will not be able to hit every ball out of his reach, either because of your own limitations or your opponent's abilities. When faced with a situation of having to return the ball, but knowing that you cannot safely play it out of range, you will have to adopt another fundamental tactic—play on your opponent's weakness.

If the person you are playing is a good friend of yours, you will probably know what are his best shots

Playing on an opponent's weakness is an important tactic in tennis. You should try to discover your opponent's weaknesses during the warm-up. Most beginners have a weaker backhand than forehand. So start playing on his backhand.

and what are his worst. So when you can't hit the ball out of range, the next best thing is to play it to your opponent's weakest shot. If you have never played against him before, you may have to assess his strengths and weaknesses during the course of the game. Generally a player's backhand is weaker than his forehand, so start the game by directing the ball to his backhand side.

Unless you are playing a very inexperienced player, your chances of being able to hit outright winners will be very few. You will have to make do with playing the ball back to your opponent's weaker side, hoping that he will make a mistake or allow you the chance of placing the ball away from him. Your best chance of doing this will be to get close to the net so that you can play an angled volley.

Unfortunately, merely charging into the net is rarely successful. The person you are playing against will simply lob the ball over your head or attempt a passing shot. It is only safe to close in on the net when you have hit a particularly difficult shot into your opponent's court. If this shot puts him under pressure, it is unlikely that he will be able to hit an adequate lob or an accurate passing shot. This then gives you your opportunity of going for the volley. A shot played to inconvenience the opponent and allow the player to come safely to the net is called an approach shot.

Of course, a player who has hit a good service that will prove difficult for his opponent to return, is in a good position to move directly up to the net. He can then angle away his opponent's effort at getting the ball back. This tactic is called serve and volley.

The surface of the court

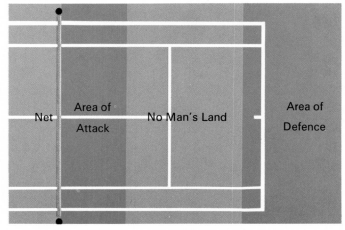

At this stage it is worth considering another factor which will almost certainly influence the tactics you decide to adopt—the court surface. Around the world tennis is played on a wide variety of surfaces and the pace and height a ball bounces will vary according to the surface. Grass, which was the original surface on which the game was played, is still common in many parts of the world. However, the expense of maintaining a grass court, and the restrictions of play imposed by the weather, are two disadvantages which have led to a decline in the use of grass courts for playing tennis. On a well-maintained grass surface the ball will bounce fairly low and fast.

Shale courts, sometimes called clay or dirt courts, are another traditional surface for playing tennis. These courts are covered with a sandy surface usually made from crushed brick, although in some countries the surface is made up from crushed ant hills! Compared with grass, shale is a slower surface and produces a higher bounce. It is much harder to hit winners on this type of court and rallies generally last longer. As with grass, this type of surface is expensive to maintain.

Besides grass and shale, there are many other types

The area between the service line and just in front of the baseline is no-man's-land. Avoid being caught in this area by advancing to the net or retreating to the baseline.

of surface on which tennis can be played. Perhaps the most common is the tarmacadam or asphalt surfaces frequently found in playgrounds and parks. The playing properties of this type of court vary widely and usually depend on the constituency of the playing surface. In recent years the demand for courts with low maintenance costs and that can be played on in all weather conditions has greatly improved the range and quality of hard surfaces. Many courts available today can be played on only minutes after heavy rain, and require the minimum of maintenance.

There are many different types of carpet surface available for indoor use. The speed and bounce of the ball can vary greatly from one type of carpet to another, and the type of material over which the carpet is laid

The grass courts below are some of the most famous in the world. These are the outer courts at the All England Club in Wimbledon. Well-kept grass courts produce a low, fast bounce.

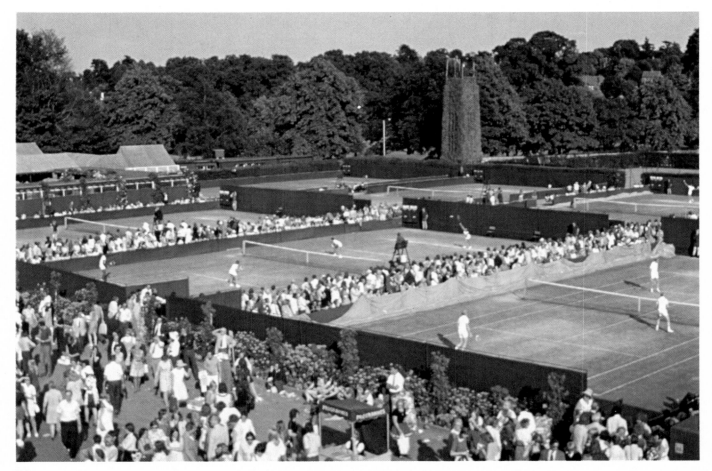

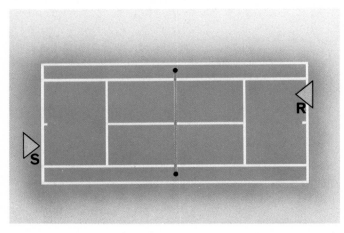

When playing singles, the server should stand as near to the centre mark as possible. This puts him in the best position to reach any return of serve.
The receiver should stand close to the baseline.

Indoor courts are generally made of wood or have a carpet surface laid over a wood or concrete floor.

Wooden courts produce a low, fast bounce but the bounce on a carpet surface will vary.

also affects the playing characteristics of these courts. Some countries have indoor courts with wooden surfaces and on these the ball bounces very fast and low.

Tactics and the singles game

Tactics are not only about where to place the ball in your opponent's half of the court, they also concern where you position yourself on your side of the net. This is apparent when considering the advantage held by a player standing close up to the net, but we have seen that it is not always possible to get close to the net without falling victim to a well-executed lob or an accurate passing shot.

When not at the net, a player's best position is back behind the baseline and in a central position. You must be prepared for a ball coming wide to the forehand or wide to the backhand, and you can be sure that your opponent will be trying to hit the ball as close to the baseline as possible. In turn, you should be aiming to return the ball as close to his baseline as is reasonably safe. If you hit the ball short and it bounces mid-court, he will have the opportunity of moving in. From mid-court he can angle his return, and follow it up to the net.

So, moving into a mid-court position to hit an approach shot is about the only time you should venture

into this territory during the course of a rally. The area between the service line and the baseline is the no-man's land of the tennis court, and should be avoided.

The right position for serving when playing singles is behind the baseline, and within a few feet of the centre mark. This will leave you in the best place to deal with your opponent's return. If you stand too far to one side or the other, you will be in difficulty if your opponent returns your service to the opposite side of the court.

The person who is receiving service should also remember that the ball could come to any part of the service box. He must be prepared to hit his return on the forehand or backhand side. The best position to receive service when playing singles is standing on the baseline 30–60 cm (1–2 ft) in from the singles side-line. You can move forward a metre (3 ft) or back a metre (3 ft) according to how hard your opponent serves. Remember, once you have hit your return of serve, you should centre-up behind the baseline, or if your shot was particularly good move up to the net.

The French and Italian championships are played on a loose sandy surface called clay or shale. These courts produce a slow, low bounce. The court in the picture is at the Stade Roland Garros in Paris.

Tactics and the doubles game

Doubles tennis is mistakenly thought by some beginners as simply a way of cramming two extra players on a tennis court when there are not enough courts for everyone to play singles. They believe that it is not a serious game, at all. In fact, doubles is a fascinating variation on the game of tennis, with many tactics and techniques all its own. Furthermore, the game of doubles introduces a complete new concept into tennis—teamwork.

Apart from requiring all the basic skills of a singles player a doubles player must be able to work in harmony with his partner. Some doubles players even develop a special sign language to enable themselves to communicate with each other on court without their opponents understanding. However, it is unlikely that you will come across such advanced methods in your early years of playing tennis.

Perhaps the first thing you should understand when starting to play doubles is when it is your turn to hit the ball and when it is your partner's. Unlike some games, table-tennis for example, doubles partners don't have to take turns to hit the ball during the course of a rally, although they do take turns in receiving service. Either partner is entitled to play the ball once the service return has been made.

As a rule in doubles each player looks after one

When the ball has been returned down the centre, it is usual for the player who can reach it with his forehand to play the ball.

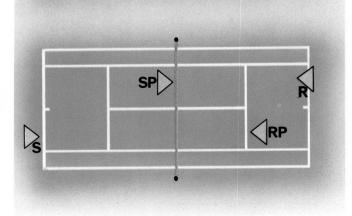

In doubles the server should stand midway between the centre mark and the doubles sideline. His partner should stand close to the net.

side of his half of the court. But when a ball is played down the middle of the court the ball should be played by the partner who last struck the ball or, if agreed beforehand, the player who can use his strongest stroke to make the return. Where there is doubt as to who should play the ball, one player, agreed beforehand, should call 'yours' or 'mine'.

At the start of each set of doubles the players must decide who will receive service in the right court and who will receive in the left court. As a rule the player in the right court will have more balls coming to his forehand, while the player in the left court will have to deal with more balls on his backhand. Generally the player with the strongest backhand receives service in the left-hand court. Of course, once a rally is in progress, one or other player can move into his partner's side of the court to play a stroke, but when this happens, the other player should cross to the side of the court that has been left unguarded.

It is poor tactics for one player to remain at the net while his opponent patrols the baseline. Both players in a doubles team should move up to the net together or back to the baseline together. This way a human wall is formed, making it difficult for the opponents to penetrate.

When playing doubles, the best position from which to serve is mid-way between the sideline and the centre mark—about a metre (3 ft) nearer the side of the court than when serving in singles. From this position you are best placed to cover any return to your side of the court, bearing in mind that your partner should deal with any balls directed to the other side of the court.

The service receiver stands in much the same position in doubles as he would when playing singles. However, if he notices that the server has moved nearer the sideline, he should adjust his position to expect a more angled delivery. If the server has moved nearer the centre mark, he will probably aim his delivery down the centre of the court.

Provided the server is reasonably competent, his partner should stand at the net, directly opposite the receiver. His job is to volley the receiver's return if it

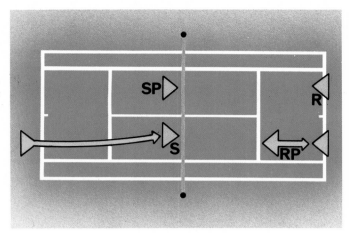

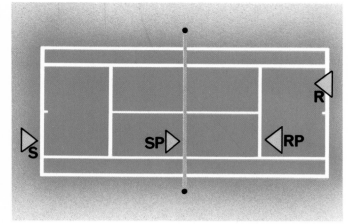

After serving, the server should move up to volley the service return.

Receiver's partner should retreat to the baseline.

When the Australian formation is used, the server's partner remains

close to the net on the same side of the court as the server.

comes within his range. The receiver's partner stands on the edge of the service box so he can move up to the net if his partner hits a good return, or back to the baseline if the return is weak.

When one of the service receivers has a particularly good cross-court service return, it is a useful tactic to position the server's partner at the net on the same side of the court as the server. In this way he is well placed to volley the cross-court return. This system is called the Australian formation.

The tactic of gaining control of the net can be understood by considering

the two net players as forming a large brick wall built across the court.

The serve-and-volley tactic used when playing singles is equally, if not more, effective when playing doubles. In a doubles match the server only has his side of the court to worry about. Once he has served, it is an easy matter for him to approach into the service box on his side of the court, placing him in a good position to volley his opponent's return of serve.

In singles play serve-and-volley tennis is generally advisable only on fast surfaces, because of the greater court area an in-coming singles player has to cover. When doubles is played by competent players, the technique is used on all court surfaces, regardless of their speed.

Practising the game

The player in the picture is practising with the help of a ball-back device. Using an aid such as the one illustrated above, or a wall, is the best method of practising when a partner is not available.

Although tennis is essentially an enjoyable and satisfying pastime, it can also have its frustrating moments, particularly if you are the type of person who likes to excel at your chosen sport. Because tennis is a game for two or more persons, it is difficult to practise unless you have a willing partner. The weather can often disrupt practice plans, and in most countries indoor facilities are rare.

If you have access to a court, but you have nobody to play with, it is a valuable opportunity to practise your service. It is advisable to get as many old balls as you can when practising the service—the more balls you have, the less time you need spend wandering about the court gathering them together.

Start practising the service with the action described in Chapter 1. When you feel you have attained a high degree of competence using this method, progress to the action described in Chapter 4. Finally you can have a go at the spin services described in Chapter 7.

It is a good idea, when practising this stroke, to serve two balls into one service box and then two into the other. If you miss the box with the first ball, try extra hard to hit the target area with the second. In this way you will recreate the conditions you experience during a game and you will feel more confident when playing in matches.

As your skill increases, place cardboard boxes or tin cans in the corners of the service boxes and try hitting them with the ball. Being able to direct your service to your opponent's forehand or backhand will be a great tactical weapon when playing in matches.

Of course, it is possible to develop the stroke actions for the forehand and backhand drive without having a partner to return the ball, but there is not much else you will be able to do singlehanded, unless you have the use of a wall, a ball-back device, or a ball-throwing machine.

A high wall, at the back of a tennis court, or even in

a yard or back garden is a great aid to a tennis player, provided there is room to swing a tennis racket and a firm flat surface on which the ball can bounce. Bjorn Borg developed his early skills by imagining he was playing tennis for Sweden, while hitting the ball up against a garage wall in his garden.

A line marking the height of the net can be chalked or painted on to the wall. With the possible exception of the lob, any stroke can be practised with the use of the wall. The service and smash actions can be developed by aiming the ball hard at the ground in front of the base of the wall. The ball will rebound off the wall coming back high over head allowing the person using the wall a chance to practise a smash action. Volleys should be practised from a position about 1·8 m (6 ft) from the wall and groundstrokes from about 6 m (20 ft) away.

When practising with a partner, groundstrokes should be hit from behind the baseline and directed to within a metre or two (1–2 yd) of the opposite baseline. A competitive element can be introduced by seeing how long you and your partner can maintain a rally. When rallying, direct the ball to both sides of your partner and get him to do the same for you. It is important to improve your weaknesses as well as building up your strong points.

The volley should be practised by one player standing up close to the net—within 1·8 m (6 ft)—while the other player hits balls to him from the baseline. After an agreed time, the player at the net can retire to the baseline while his partner has a go at the net.

The smash can be practised by one player while his partner is developing his lob. The player who is smashing should stand about mid-court while the lobber is back behind the baseline.

Before starting a game, it is customary for experienced tennis players to spend a few minutes practising the range of shots they are likely to encounter during the match. Starting with the groundstrokes, forehand and backhand, they move to the net for some volleys, retreat to the middle of the court to hit a few overheads, put up some lobs while their opponent practises his overheads, and finally hit a few services. This is a routine you would be advised to follow.

With tennis, the old adage 'Practice makes perfect' needs qualifying. Because you cannot see yourself playing, it is not always easy to know if what you are doing is correct. Practice is very important, but get a more experienced player, or coach, to check your actions are right before spending hours 'grooving' them on the tennis court.

A good system of practise when three players are available is for one player to play against the other two. Each player takes his turn to serve.

Use the warm-up period for practising your strokes. One player stands on the baseline to practise groundstrokes while the other practises volleys.

4 Adding to your repertoire

The volley

You are now finding that tennis can be more than just hitting a ball backwards and forwards across a net. Developing the tactical side of the game will not only increase your enjoyment of tennis, but also improve your chances of success. However, before you can put your knowledge of tactics into practice on the tennis court, you will need to add a few more strokes to your repertoire. In this chapter you will learn about the volley—hitting the ball before it has bounced; the smash—hitting the ball above your head; and the lob—hitting the ball over the head of your opponent. The final section of this chapter will help you to improve your service.

We have seen how a player standing at the net is well placed to control the outcome of a rally. From this position he can angle the ball out of reach of his opponent and, because he can reach the ball before it has bounced, has the advantage of catching his opponent unprepared. But the volley is a stroke many beginners try to avoid. They feel that by standing close to the net, they are in danger of being hit and, because they do not have enough time to prepare themselves, they frequently mishit the ball.

First you must conquer the fear of being hit. In fact, a tennis ball can do you very little damage however hard it is hit, unless it strikes you in the eye. Provided you always watch the ball when it is in play, you will have time to put the racket in its path, even if it is coming straight towards you.

People who find the volley difficult are usually trying to do too much. It is what you don't do, rather than what you do, that will make you a good volleyer. And, the most important *don't* is swing. To volley you use the third of the basic tennis movements—the punch. When you volley, the racket head moves in a straight line for about a metre (3 ft) in the direction you want the ball to travel. Trying to swing at a volley, the way you do when you hit your groundstrokes, is the most common mistake among people who have trouble with this stroke. So, at the net swinging is out. There is no need, and there is no time.

Unlike most other strokes in tennis it is not possible to practise the volley without a wall, ball-back equipment, a ball-thrower or someone to hit balls to you. But it is worth becoming familiar with the movements of the volley before you get involved with the additional complication of having to hit a ball. Standing in your ready position, about 2 m (6 ft) from the net, with the racket held in a continental grip, imagine a ball coming at you on your forehand side. Take the racket back so that the face of the racket is head-high and level with the right side of your body. Your racket arm should be bent and the head of your racket should not be

The backhand volley: the best position to practise the volley is about 2 m (6 ft) back from the net.

When volleying it is more important than ever to adopt a good ready position.

For the backhand volley the player takes the racket back so that the head is just above and just behind

the left shoulder. This is a bit further back than for the forehand volley.

 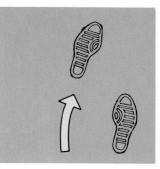 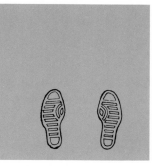 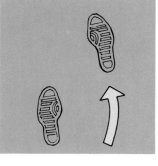

For the forehand volley the player steps forward with the left foot as he moves the racket.

The step should be short and in the direction of the net, bringing the player's body sideways.

For the backhand volley the player steps forward with his right foot as the ball approaches.

Note that the movement of the foot is forward and not diagonally across.

more than 50 cm (18 in) away from your right shoulder. Step with your left foot in the direction of the net, moving the racket head through the air in a straight line in the direction you want the ball to travel. As with the groundstrokes, the point of contact with the ball should be level with your leading foot, your wrist should be firm on impact and your knees bent. The follow-through of the racket head after impact should continue a short distance along the same line that the racket travelled to meet the ball.

Because there is less time to prepare for volleys, there is seldom time to adjust the grip for the forehand or backhand stroke. It is best, therefore, when standing up close to the net, to use the continental grip, which is adequate for volleying on either side of our body.

The backhand volley is a similar stroke to the forehand variety. The racket face is brought back head-high and level with the left-hand side of your body. Step forward with your right foot as the ball approaches and punch the racket head at the ball at the angle you wish the ball to travel. The follow-through should continue a short distance along the line that the ball has been directed. Some players prefer to increase their backswing and follow-through slightly on the backhand volley.

Practise the stroke with a friend hitting the ball to your forehand side. Once you have mastered the forehand volley, get him to 'feed' your backhand stroke. Finish up with your friend alternating his feed to your forehand and backhand, an exercise that will greatly improve your footwork on this stroke.

As the ball approaches, the player steps forward with his right foot and punches the racket head at the ball.

The racket head should move to the ball in a straight line not an arc.

When volleying, the racket head finishes chest-high and pointing to the far end of the court. The player's

arm is fully extended in the direction he has angled his shot.

The smash

One of the most impressive sights when watching top tennis players in action is the way they handle high balls above their heads. The stroke they use in this situation is called the smash—here the player seems to rise above the court like a salmon leaping for a fly, and powers the ball into the furthest corner of the court. Seldom do they miss and rarely do their opponents manage to return the ball.

However, as is often the case when watching experts, it looks simple when they do it but when we try it ourselves, we find it is not so easy. Fortunately, you have already learnt how to tackle this stroke, although you may not realize it. In fact, the smash is almost exactly the same action as the overhead service.

As with the service, the smash is a throwing movement. You use the continental grip, and you stand sideways to the net when hitting the ball. Of course, you cannot control the position of the ball when smashing as that is up to your opponent, so you must adjust your own position in relation to the ball. This will often require running backwards or sideways.

Moving to a correct position to hit the smash is the most difficult part of this stroke, and failure to get in a good position is the most common mistake among beginners. When smashing, the ball should be about 1–1·2 m (3–4 ft) above your head, and in line with the front of your left foot. This is exactly the same position, in relation to your body, as when you are serving.

When attempting a smash, there is a great tendency to look away from the ball a moment or two before impact. There is a temptation to look where your opponent is standing because you want to place the ball out of his reach, or you are afraid of hitting him. Not watching the ball on to the racket during the smash will often result in a mishit.

The lob

The purpose of the lob is simply to get the ball back high and, hopefully, over the head of your opponent. Often it is a stroke played in desperation when you are under pressure and can only just get your racket to the ball. In this situation there is little time to prepare for the stroke, so the backswing is short and the follow-through is long. As with the serve, the lob is a variation of a stroke we have already learned—or rather two strokes we have learned—the forehand drive and the backhand drive.

When lobbing, use the same grip as you would for

The action of the smash is very similar to that of the service. The racket head has started to move up from the backscratcher position and the player's left arm is pointing at the ball.

The racket face should meet the ball slightly to the fore of the player with the player's arm at full stretch above his head. The racket will follow through across the player's body.

your drives—the eastern forehand or the eastern backhand, depending on which side of you the ball is bouncing. But take the racket head back only half as far as you would for hitting your groundstrokes. The head of your racket should be just above knee-height and pointing to the side of the court. As you take the racket back, swivel on the balls of your feet. Step forward and across with your foot (left for forehand, right for backhand lob), making sure your knees are well bent. When lobbing, you are hitting under the ball, so your body must be lower for this stroke. From this position your racket head should swing down and up underneath the ball. The face of the racket should be angled towards the sky on impact and the point of contact should be on the underneath side of the ball. Follow through vertically into the air with the racket head finishing high and pointing to the sky, but on the same side of your body as you have struck the ball.

The action of the lob is more leisurely than that of the groundstroke. The swing should be slower and the ball should remain on the strings longer—it is almost a scooping movement. Because the follow-through is almost vertical and not as fast as the follow-through on the groundstrokes, the back foot will not automatically swing round to a position alongside the leading foot. So after lobbing you should make a more conscious effort to return to the ready position.

Above A lob should be played when your opponent has approached too close to the net.

Below The lob is very similar to the forehand drive although the back-swing for the lob is shorter.

The player moves his feet in exactly the same way as he would to hit a drive on the forehand side.

The racket finishes high in the air and on the right-hand side of his body

Improving your service

At this stage it is worth taking a second look at the service. You will remember that when playing tennis every point is begun by one player or the other putting the ball in play—serving. In fact, the service is the only stroke you *have* to make when playing tennis. If your backhand is weak, you can run around it so that everything comes to your forehand. If your volley is weak, you can stay at the baseline—there are many successful tennis players who never come to the net to volley. But if your service is poor, that's tough, because your game will suffer badly.

The good thing about the service is that it is entirely up to you. If you mess it up, you have only yourself to blame. It is the only time, when playing tennis, that you are completely in control of what happens to the ball. The choice is yours, whether you serve to your opponent's forehand or backhand, whether you serve hard or soft, or whether to spin your service or hit it flat. In every other instance during a game the ball will have been hit to you by an opponent trying to make it as difficult as possible for you to return.

Because the server has the initiative when playing tennis, he should win his service games. It is therefore doubly important to develop a reliable service. So far, you have learnt how to hit a good basic service

which incorporates many of the features top players use when they serve—the throwing action, the continental grip, the positioning of the feet and the throw-up. But the time has now come to take the serve a little further.

Stand behind the baseline in your correct service position, with the racket held in a continental grip. The racket head should be shoulder-high and pointing towards the net. Your racket arm should be bent at the elbow and held about 10 cm (4 in) in front of your stomach. Now, let your racket arm go completely limp. It should drop down beside you with the racket head pointing at the floor.

Try this movement a couple of times. If you are really letting your arm go limp, you should find that your wrist, which is turned in towards your body when the racket is being held up, turns outwards as the racket drops down by your leg. You should also find that the racket swings past your leg rather like the pendulum of a clock.

Now try the same dropping action with the racket arm, this time continuing the pendulum swing past your leg and up, so that the racket arm finishes extended behind you at shoulder-height. Next, bend your elbow fully. This action will bring the racket head back behind your left shoulder blade, and into what is often known as the backscratcher position. You should now be standing in exactly the position you have been adopting for the simple service described in Chapter 1.

When serving, the player takes up his position behind the baseline. His feet are placed comfortably apart.

The player drops the racket arm down and at the same time drops the left arm. The right arm swings past his leg like a pendulum.

The player continues to take his racket back at the same time throwing up the ball with his left hand.

With all this pendulum swinging and backscratching going on, the service is becoming a rather complicated operation, although in reality it is much simpler than it sounds. Now that we have sorted out the function of your right arm in the service, what about the left?

You will remember that we use the left arm for throwing up the ball to serve. Starting with the racket gripped in the right hand, with the racket head held shoulder-high and pointing towards the net, hold the ball with the left hand so that it is touching the face of the racket. Now, drop your racket arm as you did for the pendulum swing, at the same time dropping your left arm. Then, as your right hand begins its upwards movement for the back half of the pendulum swing, start moving your left hand up for the throw-up. So, when serving, both hands should drop down together and both hands should rise together. Developing this action will help your co-ordination, rhythm and timing.

Your service action should now be resembling that of a top-class player, although it is unlikely that it will be as effective as Borg's or Connors's quite yet. But before leaving the serve and moving on to other things, one further refinement will help improve the success of your serve. As your hands drop, push your bottom out—not too much, but enough to put your weight on the heels of your feet. Then, as your hands start their upward journey, push your hips forward, thus shifting your weight on to the balls of your feet.

Above When hitting a service the racket head should be thrown at the ball from a backscratcher position.

Bending the elbow of his right arm the player brings the head of the racket back behind his left shoulder-blade.

The player is fully stretched and on his toes when the racket makes contact with the ball. His shoulders are square to the net.

The follow-through for the service is across the player's body and down past the outside of his leg.

5 Learning from watching others

One way of learning how to do something is by watching someone else doing it. When tennis coaches are trained, they are always taught to demonstrate the stroke or point they are coaching, as well as explaining it in detail.

What better way to improve your game than by seeing the world's best tennis players in action? This can be done by visiting a tournament—most parts of the world hold at least one major tennis tournament each year—or by watching a match on the television.

Television can be a great help to anyone learning how to play the game, especially when the pictures are accompanied by a knowledgeable commentary. However, in most television coverage of tennis the camera follows the ball back and forth, so the viewer never gets a chance to see the preparation a player makes before hitting the ball, or the follow-through after the ball has been hit.

When watching a tennis match live, you have to be your own camera man and commentator. There is so much going on at a tennis match that you will have to

Chris Evert has reached the end of the follow- through on her famous two-handed backhand.

Above Australia's Evonne Cawley prepares to hit a sliced backhand.

Right Bjorn Borg has a two-handed backhand and hits forehand with topspin.

'zoom in' on one particular aspect of the game if you are to gain any advantage from being there. Most people who watch tennis simply follow the ball up and down the court, keep check on the score and hope that the player they like best will win.

To gain the greatest benefit from visiting a tennis tournament, you will have to detach yourself from the drama taking place on court. Select one of the players and concentrate on him for a while. To do this you will have to ignore the ball. Note the way he grips his racket and look carefully to see whether he uses a different grip to hit his backhand. Watch the way he holds his racket when serving.

Shift your focus to his feet. See the different ways he positions his feet for the service, the groundstrokes and the volleys. Note the way he moves his feet when running to get a 'wide' ball—his steps should be short and quick. Watch the way he runs back when hitting an overhead and note how much time he spends on his toes ready to spring into action when the ball comes to his side of the net. When you feel you have learned something about a tennis player's footwork, switch your attention to his racket.

Study the way in which your player swings his racket when hitting a groundstroke. Note how early he takes the racket back in preparation for the stroke.

Britain's Sue Barker uses a western grip when hitting the forehand drive. It is an unusual style among top-class players. Sue was born in Paignton, Devon on the 19 April 1956.

Try to put yourself in his position and see if he has adopted any special tactics to deal with his opponent. Is he directing the ball to his opponent's backhand? Perhaps he is trying to tire him out by making him run about the court? Is he hitting the ball hard—playing the power game—or is he soft-balling the man on the other side of the net? Is he using spin to gain the advantage, and if so is it topspin or slice?

Watch carefully the way he serves and note where he stands. Does he direct his service across to the side of the court or straight down the centre? How does his first serve differ from the second? Most professional players use a topspin second serve, so see whether the ball kicks up high when landing in his opponent's service box. Does he move to the net directly he has served so that his next stroke is a volley? If so, note whether he is inside the service line to play his first volley.

When you have considered all these factors about one player, use the same method of analysis on his opponent. Of course, not everything you will see will be good. Even the best players make mistakes. When a player loses a point, try to diagnose the fault. Think what he should have done to have taken the advantage.

There is a third side to every tennis match. We have considered the technical side—the techniques the players use to control the ball, and we have thought

Left-handed Jimmy Connors uses a two-handed grip for his backhand. He slices the ball on both sides.

Try to judge whether he is hitting the ball as it is falling after reaching the full height of the bounce, or whether he strikes it 'on the rise'. Where does the racket end up after the ball has been struck? See how little movement of the racket there is when a top player hits a volley and note the way the racket drops down behind a player into a backscratcher position when he hits an overhead or service.

By concentrating on an individual player in this way for the duration of several games, you will have built up a store of information about the technique he uses for hitting the ball. But, while the technical side of a player's game is very important, there are many other aspects of tennis you can learn from watching a top-class player.

Consider the tactical angle of your player's game. Start by noticing where he stands when he is receiving service. Does he stand in front of or behind the baseline? Does he move in when his opponent misses his first service? Note whether he is a baseliner or a volleyer. Does he prefer to stay back, contesting the point from the back of the court, or does he move forward into a volleying position at the earliest opportunity? Remember that his tactics will be influenced by the type of court on which the match is being played.

48

becoming over-cautious, staying back on the baseline, never venturing up to volley. This change of tactics will almost certainly be to his opponent's advantage. He will see that the man on the other side of the net is experiencing a crisis of confidence and will try to exploit the situation.

So the player who starts with the psychological advantage could soon find the match turning against him. On the other hand, consider the man who has come on court knowing that everyone expects him to get beaten. He has nothing to lose, but everything to gain.

Once the game has begun, study the way the players react to pressure points. These are the points which, if a player wins or loses, will mean he wins or loses a game, a set or the match. Note which player is confident in these situations, taking risks and going for winners. Alternatively, look out for signs of nervousness. Many players become hesitant at critical moments, getting ultra-cautious and playing safe. Watch for signs of tension—missing easy shots, arguing with the officials. These are signs of a bad match-temperament. It is often the player who remains calm, even when defeat looks certain, who fights his way back and wins in the end.

Although a great deal of good can be gained from

Billie Jean King will be remembered as one of the greatest women players. She has campaigned tirelessly in the cause of women's tennis.

about the tactics—the thinking part of playing tennis. The third factor, which may have the greatest influence on the outcome of the match, is the psychological side. A tennis match is not only a contest of skill and wit, but a psychological battle as well. Understanding the psychological battle that takes place on court is unlikely to help your game when you play your friends at school or in the park. But it could help you appreciate why a player with superior tactics and technique can get beaten.

The mental conflict begins the moment the players walk out on court. Usually there is a favourite at the start of any tennis match—one player generally has a better record of wins, or is particularly on form. This player *should* be confident—he *should* have the psychological advantage to start the match. This may make him self assured. He will go for his shots, play attacking tennis and take his chances when they come. If, however, he becomes careless, he might begin to worry. The thought of being beaten by a 'lesser' player could spoil his reputation.

Once a player starts thinking in this negative way, he may become tentative, scared to hit the ball hard in case it goes out. He begins to play defensive tennis,

Vitas Gerulaitis has the reputation of being a playboy, although he is one of the finest tennis players around today.

watching players more experienced than yourself, it can also do a great deal of harm. Many beginners visit a tournament or watch a professional match on television and believe that they can go on court and play in exactly the same way as the stars. When their results are disappointing, they become disillusioned and lose interest in the game.

When watching the top players in action, it is important to realize what has gone into their games. The technique they use has been developed over many years. Most of today's best players started intensive training before they were ten years old. Many of them were playing regularly at four or five. Their styles have been carefully developed by the top coaches in their countries. You mustn't think that you will able to play like them after a few weeks' practice, or even a few years' practice. Trying to run before you can walk is a common error. It has been the downfall of many a promising young player. Developing a winning technique must be done step by step.

Trying to imitate the advanced technique of the professionals is one thing that should be avoided. Don't spend hours practising the topspin lob when you haven't mastered the flat forehand drive. You would hardly expect to succeed with calculus before

Left Virginia Wade stoops low to play a half-volley on the backhand side. Virginia won Wimbledon in 1977.

Below Pam Shriver prepares to hit an overhead. Note the way her left hand is held up in the air.

Martina Navratilova, who was born in Czechoslovakia, is one of the many gifted players to come from East Europe.

Martina won Wimbledon in 1979. A left-handed player, she is noted for her aggressive attitude and eagerness to attack.

you had learnt your three-times table. Another common mistake is to think that acting, or even dressing, like your favourite player will improve your game.

Many talented players in the public eye behave impeccably when on court. Unfortunately, the antics of a few skilful players are deplorable. Remember, players like Ilie Nastase and John McEnroe have triumphed in tennis, despite their temperaments. Throwing a tantrum, or your racket, is more likely to upset *your* game than that of your opponent. Displaying your emotions will only make your opponent think you are cracking up and strengthen his resolve to win.

Don't be alarmed when you see a famous player hitting the ball or holding the racket in a way different from the one you have been taught. In fact, there is no *one* way to do anything in tennis. Every year a new player emerges who does something in an unorthodox fashion. Nowadays tennis instructors like to encourage players to innovate. Natural techniques—provided they are successful—are developed.

Once upon a time a player like Bjorn Borg would have been taught to stand sideways to the net to hit a forehand drive, and to use only one hand on the backhand. This might have made him a more elegant player, but perhaps he would have lost all his power. Bjorn Borg's coach could see the natural strengths of the young Swede's game and concentrated on improving the boy's weaknesses.

Remember, what might be right for Borg might not be right for you. The standard techniques taught by tennis instructors are based on the most successful styles of the players in the last hundred-odd years. But there are often many ways of getting to the same place. Teaching someone to play tennis is rather like giving directions to a stranger who has stopped to ask the way in your neighbourhood. If you tell him all the different routes he could take, he will probably get confused and end up lost.

Visiting a tennis tournament for the first time can be a bewildering experience, even to someone familiar with the way the game is played. Understanding how a tournament is organized will add greatly to your enjoyment. Most tournaments have 16, 32, 64, or in the case of the really big ones, 128 players taking part. All of the major tournaments are graded according to the amount of money that is being offered in prizes. Besides winning prize-money in a tournament, a player can win points, according to how well he does. The results of the world's leading 200 players are fed into a computer, and each player is given a world ranking according to the points he has gained in the previous twelve months.

A player's position on the world ranking list will decide whether he can enter a particular tournament and whether he is given a special position in the draw. The draw is the method of deciding who plays who in the opening round, and the names of all the players taking part in the tournament are put in a hat and drawn out. The best four, eight or sixteen players, depending on the size of the tournament, are given special positions before the draw is made, so that they do not play against each other in the early rounds. This process is called seeding. At one time the seeded players in a tournament were decided upon by a committee formed by the tournament organizers. Nowadays, a player is seeded according to his place on the computer rankings. Usually there is a large board at a tournament showing the draw and indicating the seeded players. This information is also included in the official programmes at most tournaments.

Although most of the players accepted by the organizers to play in their tournament are chosen according to their position on the computer ranking list, many tournaments reserve a few places for 'qualifiers'. This means that another tournament is held before the main one begins. This lesser tournament is usually referred to as the 'qualifying', and the players who do best in this event are allowed a place in the main tournament.

To organize a tennis tournament requires a great many officials and helpers. A fully staffed tennis court has thirteen officials and six ballboys. The officials consist of an umpire who sits on a high-chair a short distance from the net post, a net-cord judge who sits close by the net post with one finger on the top of the net so he can feel whether the ball clips the net during

Above Roscoe Tanner, a left-hander from Tennessee, is famous for the speed of his service.

Right Ilie Nastase is one of the finest touch players. However, he has a fiery temperament.

a service, a foot-fault judge who moves from one baseline to the other according to which end the service is, and ten line-judges positioned around the court. Four ballboys stand at the corners of the court to supply the server with balls, and two more crouch by the net post to gather the balls that go in the net.

The umpire has overall charge of the match and can overrule any of the line-judges if he feels they have made a mistake. When a ball looks out and the line-judge has not called it, the umpire will look across to the line-judge to check the situation. If the line-judge holds his hand up to his eyes, it means he was unsighted and could not see whether the ball was in or out. Should a player feel he has been unfairly treated by the umpire, he can ask for the tournament referee to be called. The referee can overrule the umpire, but will only do so in extreme cases.

Every tennis match is started with new balls, and these are changed after seven games and then after every nine. New balls are kept in a refrigerated box by the umpire's chair. The new balls will be much livelier than the ones that have been in play for six games, and whoever serves first with the new balls has a big advantage.

Something that you will probably come across when watching tournament tennis, but which you are unlikely to encounter in your early days of playing, is the tie-break. This is a fairly recent introduction to the game of tennis and is a method of limiting the length of a match. There are two main tie-break systems in existence—the 9-point tie-break and the 12-point tie-break—and it is up to the tournament organizers whether they use a tie-break at all and, if so, which system.

A tie-break is used to decide the winner of a set when the game scores are level—generally at 6-all or 8-all. Tournament organizers can decide whether a tie-break should be played in every set, or in all but the final set.

In a 9-point tie-break the player whose turn it is to serve serves for two points. His opponent then serves for two points and the players then change ends. The first player serves another two points, and so on until one player has won five points. The first player to win five points in this system is the winner.

The 12-point tie-break differs in that a player must be two points ahead before he can win the tie-break. Provided he has a two-point lead, the first player to reach seven points is the winner. If a player reaches

Left Left-hander John McEnroe is well known for his sliced service. At 17 he reached the quarter-finals at Wimbledon.

Below Britain's John Lloyd was a member of the Davis Cup team that reached the final in 1978. Here he prepares to serve.

Tracy Austin has a two-handed backhand, common among players who take up the game early.

seven points and is only one point ahead of his opponent the tie-break continues until one or other player is two points ahead.

During a 12-point tie-break the player whose turn it is to serve serves for one point. His opponent then serves two points and, thereafter, the service changes every two points. When the combined scores add up to six, the players change ends and then after every six points.

Much can be learnt from the way experienced players warm up before starting a match. They will start by hitting gentle forehand and backhand drives the length of the court, then one player will move up to the net to hit a few volleys. After a while the player at the net will move back to the baseline and his opponent will come forward to volley. Next, one of the players will take up a position in mid-court, while the other player hits a few lobs from the baseline. The player in mid-court takes this opportunity to warm up on his overheads. Then the player who has been smashing starts hitting lobs for his opponent to practise smashing. Finally, both players retire behind their respective baselines to practise a few serves.

This routine reduces the likelihood of any pulled muscles or strains during the game, familiarizes the player with the court surface and helps him get quickly into the natural rhythm of his game.

6 Equipment and etiquette

Buying a racket

Probably your first big expenditure when you take up tennis will be buying a racket. Many people begin playing with a racket handed down from an older brother or sister, or one found in the loft or attic. Of course, it is common sense not to rush out and spend a lot of money on equipment before you have decided whether tennis is the game for you. However, once you have made up your mind that you intend taking the game seriously, you should make sure you are properly equipped. Somebody else's racket may be entirely wrong for you and could lead to the development of bad habits when playing and even result in injury.

Nowadays there is a bewildering selection of rackets on the market covering a wide price range. It is, therefore, most important for a beginner to go about buying his first racket in the right way.

The most obvious difference in the rackets you will find on sale at sports shops is in the material from which they are made. At one time all rackets were made from wood and this is still the most popular material for making rackets today. However, the last twenty years has seen a rapid growth in the popularity of metal-frame rackets and the introduction of many new materials for racket construction, chief among these being glass-fibre and carbon-graphite.

All but the cheapest wooden rackets are made from layers of wood glued together. Often a racket will contain several different types of wood which have been selected to give it the correct blend of playing characteristics and durability. Maple, beech and ash are commonly used in racket manufacture.

The layering and the use of different types of wood give the racket frame a degree of flexibility. This absorbs the impact of the ball and helps to improve the player's control. A racket frame made from one type of wood would be too rigid or too flexible according to the type of wood used. A very rigid frame would jar on impact with the ball, putting increased strain on the racket and possibly causing injury to

There is a wide range of rackets available today. Picking the right one is an important step for a beginner.

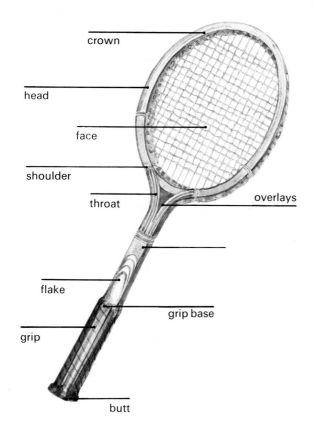

crown

head

face

shoulder

throat

overlays

flake

grip base

grip

butt

A typical wooden racket and the technical terms used to describe the various parts. It is useful to know these terms when buying a new racket.

the player's wrist or elbow. Too flexible a racket would reduce the player's control over the ball.

Metal rackets vary in playing characteristics and durability according to the composition of the metal and the method of construction. As with wooden rackets, the metal varieties come in varying degrees of flexibility. The cheapest metal brands can be very whippy, tending to snap at any welded joints. The handles on the cheaper metal models are often made from plastic and sometimes disintegrate with heavy use.

Composite rackets are new on the market and are still at an experimental stage. Although attractively designed, this type of racket is fairly expensive and offers little advantage in performance.

Having decided on the type of racket you want to buy, it is essential to get a racket that is right for you. The two most important considerations when selecting a racket from your chosen range are the weight and grip size. Most makes of racket are available in three different weights—top, medium and light—and this will be stamped on the handle. Rackets vary in weight from about 350 g (12 oz) to about 400 g (14 oz), but it is worth noting that the top racket in one manufacturer's range may not be the same weight as top in a different range. This, too, applies to medium and light rackets. There are no absolute guidelines as to the correct weight of racket for your height or build, so try to choose one that you feel comfortable with.

Rackets are also available in a variety of grip sizes. Again, most manufacturers stamp the grip size of a racket on its handle, and this will be either a measurement in inches, or a code number. The following grip sizes are generally available in most ranges of rackets: $4\frac{1}{4}$ (2), $4\frac{3}{8}$ (3), $4\frac{1}{2}$ (4), $4\frac{5}{8}$ (5), $4\frac{3}{4}$ (6), $4\frac{7}{8}$ (7). In fact, the measurement in inches is the circumference of the handle before the grip has been added. The numbers in brackets refer to a code used by some manufacturers and correspond with the measurements they follow.

You can get an approximate idea of the grip size that would best suit you by measuring the distance from the tip of your third or ring finger to the long crease that runs across your palm—this measurement should coincide with the inch-size of your racket grip. When gripping the racket correctly, there should be about a finger width of space between the tips of your fingers and the heel of your thumb.

Finally you will have to decide whether you want a racket with gut or synthetic strings. Gut has greater elasticity and allows the player more control when hitting the ball. But gut strings are more expensive than the synthetic variety, and if used in damp conditions may rot and eventually break, making an expensive re-string necessary. Although synthetic strings do not allow the same ball control as the gut variety, they cost less initially and invariably last longer. Most tournament players have at least two rackets, one strung in gut for fine weather play and one strung in with a synthetic string for use in damp conditions.

When buying new tennis balls, check that they are officially recognized by your national association. Also look for the date, which should be on the box in case they are last year's balls. If left in shops too long, balls tend to go soft.

Measure your hand as shown to find your correct grip size before choosing a racket.

$4\frac{5}{8}$ in grip size 5

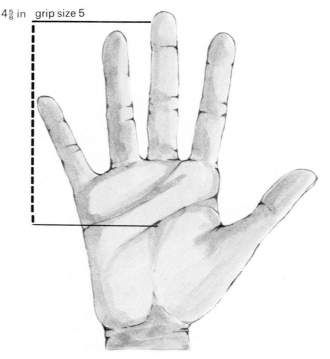

What to wear

There is nothing in the rule book about the correct clothing for playing tennis. Your tennis wear should be dictated by common sense, but will almost certainly be influenced by convention and fashion. While the official rule book does not stipulate dress requirements, you may find that the authority that manages the court on which you intend playing will have its own tennis-wear regulations, even if these only specify that soft shoes must be worn. It is well worth finding out if there are any special dress requirements in force at whatever courts you plan to use before picking your tennis wardrobe.

Shoes are an important but often neglected item of a tennis player's equipment. Make sure that you specify tennis shoes when you go into a shop, because many of the shoes made for jogging or squash, although similar in design to popular tennis shoes, have soles that would damage a tennis court. When buying tennis shoes, you will be able to choose between canvas uppers or leather uppers. Shoes with leather uppers are usually more comfortable and, of course,

more expensive. Remember that it is often the sole that wears out first, and the soles of an expensive pair of leather shoes will wear out just as quickly as the soles of a cheap pair of canvas shoes.

At one time tennis players would buy their shoes half a size too large and wear two pairs of socks. This was to cushion their feet, particularly when playing on hard surfaces. Today this is not necessary as most tennis shoes, canvas or leather, have padded insoles, tongues and collars. Make sure the shoes you buy are the right size. Ill-fitting shoes are not only uncomfortable but may result in long-term or even permanent injury.

Shorts and short-sleeved shirts are generally considered to be the most practical tennis wear for men. Before World War II most male tennis players wore long trousers, but these would almost certainly have been restricting and most uncomfortable in warm weather. Girls should wear short skirts and light-weight tops, or short dresses. Many girls prefer to wear bobble-socks when playing tennis—these come

Nowadays most sports shops offer a confusing array of equipment. Check up on the rules of dress at your courts before buying your tennis wear.

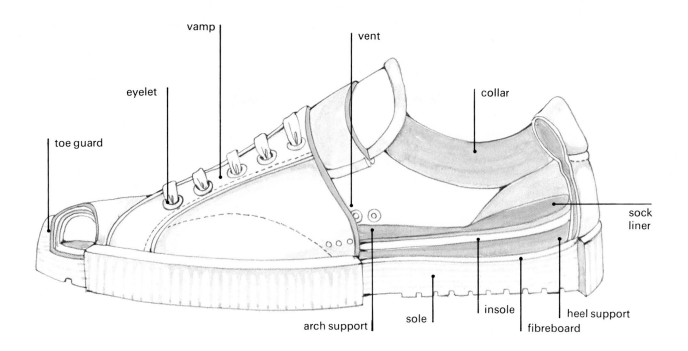

vamp | vent | collar | eyelet | toe guard | sock liner | arch support | sole | insole | fibreboard | heel support

Above and below Choose your shoes carefully making sure that they are a good fit.

just above the collar of the shoe and a bobble stitched to the back of the sock prevents it slipping down inside the shoe.

A sweater should be worn between matches or practice sessions on a warm day, and a tracksuit (sometimes called a warm-up suit) is advisable when playing on a cool day. Sweat bands can be worn on the wrist to prevent the palms getting too clammy, which would result in the racket slipping, and head bands, to prevent hair, or sweat, getting in the eyes.

Apart from the practical considerations which affect a player's choice of clothing, you may encounter dress regulations which require players to wear all white. One can understand the need to wear shoes that do not damage the court, and it is obvious that shorts are more suitable than jeans. But with the wide range of tennis clothes now available in attractive colours, it seems a shame that some tennis authorities rule that only white tennis clothes can be worn on courts under their control. Some clubs even specify that tracksuits and sweaters—if they are to be worn on court—must also be white. Clothing and shoes with coloured borders, stripes or designs are banned. However, at most clubs, even where an all-white rule exists, do not object to coloured motifs or accessories, provided that the outfit is predominantly white. When playing at courts you have not used before, check for any special dress requirements before setting out. Or take an all-white outfit along with you, just in case.

Besides dress requirements, some authorities have a code of conduct for players when using their courts. In public parks these may only concern the times when you are allowed to play and the treatment of the court, the net and the surround. But most clubs have extensive rules. If joining a new club or visiting the club of a friend, it is important to familiarize yourself with the club rules.

Tracksuits are a useful part of your tennis outfit for wearing in between matches.

Behaviour on court

In general, behaviour on court should be governed by consideration for others. When it is your opponent's turn to serve and there are balls lying about on your side of the net, gather them up and hit them down towards your opponent, making sure he knows they are coming.

Before moving on to a court, check that you are entitled to do so. There may be people who have been waiting longer than you and have a better claim to the court. When people are waiting, don't over-run your allotted time—and if you are in the middle of a game when your time runs out, check with those who are waiting before continuing to the end of the game. Spare a thought for other players in the vicinity. Don't walk across, or behind another court where there is play in progress. Wait until there is a break in play.

When you are serving, allow your opponent time to get into position before you serve. If your first service is a fault, allow time for your opponent to prepare himself before making your second delivery. When you are receiving and your opponent's first service is a fault, don't hit the ball back across the net to him. Instead direct the ball down into the bottom of the net. Remember to call clearly when your opponent's service is out, as he may not be able to see from his service position. If you are not ready and prepared to receive your opponent's serve, hold one hand up in the air so that he is aware of the situation, keeping your hand up until you are ready to continue.

Keep track of the score when playing tennis and call it out between each point. Not knowing the score will affect the way you play and will convey a lack of interest to your opponent.

When playing a social game, avoid hitting the ball directly at an opponent. Should your shot strike him, apologize immediately. When playing in competition, and court officials or ball boys are participating, take time to thank them after the match.

Always be courteous on court. Think of the space by the net post as a door and stand back so that your opponent can come through first. When you are playing doubles let your partner go first.

Always respect the facilities that you are using when playing tennis. Nets are expensive and can easily be broken if swung on or climbed over.

Above At the end of the game it is good manners to shake hands with your opponent and thank him for playing with you. In doubles shake hands with your partner first.

Right If you have been playing in a match and there has been an umpire present, shake hands with him and thank him for the work he has done.

When changing ends, think of the area beside the net post as a door and allow your opponent to go through first. Compliment your opponent on his good shots, and if he hits a lucky one, refrain from making sarcastic comments. When playing doubles, encourage your partner—this is not only good manners but also sound tactics.

If you are unsure whether a ball was in or out, give your opponent the benefit of the doubt—or suggest you play the point again. Shake hands with your opponent after the match, and when playing doubles, shake hands with your partner as well.

When your opponent, or the club, has supplied the balls, don't leave them lying about on the court after you have finished playing—help gather them up. Finally, if no one else is waiting to use the court, slacken the net and lift the bottom of the net up over the net cord. This reduces the strain on the cord and prevents the bottom of the net wearing itself out on the court surface.

Remember, to play tennis you need people to play with. If you behave selfishly on court, you could end up with no one to play with.

7 More advanced strokes

The effect of spin on a ball

One of the perplexing moments you may experience as you begin playing with people of better standards is your first topspin service. Your opponent has missed his first service and has hit his second serve high over the net and not very hard. But, as you line up to return the ball with a forehand drive, it bounces high over your left shoulder.

A tennis ball can spin in many different ways and its behaviour will vary according to the direction it is rotating. You can easily check this yourself—all you need is a tennis ball and a fairly firm floor. Holding the ball in the palm of your right hand, with your knuckles facing the ground, toss the ball forward a short distance, flicking up hard with your fingers as the ball leaves your hand. The ball will appear to accelerate away when it bounces. This type of movement is called topspin. The ball is spinning away from you, rotating in the same direction as the wheels of a car as it is being driven forward.

If the spin is in the opposite direction, it is called underspin. Holding the ball in the palm of your hand with the knuckles pointing up to the sky, toss the ball forward a short distance, flicking down with your fingertips as the ball leaves your hand. This time the ball is spinning towards you as it travels forward. On bouncing the ball will appear to decelerate, or even bounce back a little. A ball can also spin sideways as it travels through the air. This is known as sidespin, and the ball will veer away sharply on landing.

Apart from changing the way a ball bounces, spin will also affect the way a ball flies through the air. A ball hit with topspin will come to earth quickly, as if drawn to the court by a magnetic force. On the other hand, a ball hit with underspin will appear to glide through the air, showing little inclination of returning to earth. A ball hit with sidespin will curve through the air, either to right or to left, according to the direction in which the ball is rotating.

Of course, a ball is seldom hit so that the spin is exactly from top to bottom, or from one side to the other. Often a ball travels through the air with a combination of topspin and sidespin, or underspin and sidespin. The flight path of the ball and the way it bounces will vary accordingly. This type of spin is called slice.

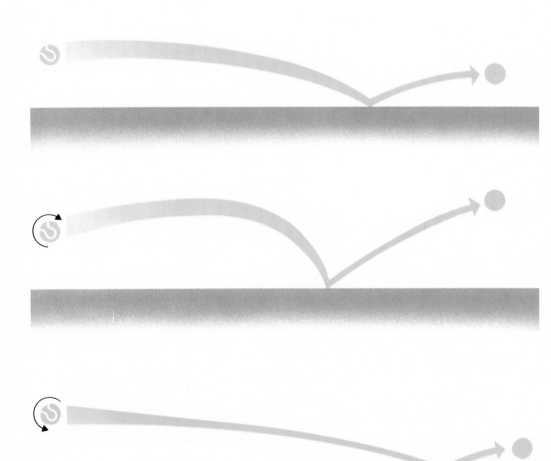

Left The diagrams on the left illustrate the effect of spin on a moving ball. The top diagram shows the flight and bounce of a ball that is moving without spin. The centre diagram shows a ball travelling with topspin—this ball will come to earth sharply and kick high on bouncing. The ball in the bottom diagram is travelling with underspin—it will float through the air and stay low on bouncing. The black arrows indicate the direction in which the ball will rotate.

Right The player is hitting a sliced forehand. Sliced strokes are useful when playing high-bouncing balls. Here the ball is chest-high as the player makes contact with his racket.

Topspin groundstrokes

It is essential that you have mastered the flat forehand drive and the flat backhand drive before you attempt to hit these shots with spin. However, the technique requires only a slight variation to the normal flat strokes, and with a few small adjustments you can learn to hit with slice and topspin.

Before explaining the changes in technique required to achieve spin, it is worth considering what actually happens when you hit a tennis ball. Most people imagine, when they start playing tennis, that the ball leaves the face of the racket immediately after impact—the way a ball bounces off a brick wall. In fact, the ball stays on the face of the racket for quite a long time—it is carried along by the strings. This is particularly true when the ball makes contact with the 'sweet spot' of the racket, as it will then sink into the strings in the way that a gymnast sinks into a trampoline.

When making a stroke, there is a point when the ball makes contact with the strings, and a point, a little while later, when it leaves the strings. This explains why the correct follow-through is so important. It is the way a racket face leaves the ball, not the way that it meets the ball, which causes spin. When the strings slide up the back and across the top of the ball, the ball will travel with topspin. When they slide down the back and along the bottom, the ball will travel with underspin. So, to hit a forehand drive with topspin, you have to adjust your basic flat stroke so that, after impact, the strings of your racket travel up the back of the ball and across the top before the racket head and the ball go their separate ways.

Holding the racket in an eastern forehand grip and starting from your ready position, take the racket head back as you would for your forehand drive. Turn sideways to the net by stepping across with your left foot. Start swinging forward, getting the racket head well down so that it is only a short distance from the ground. This should be done by

Standing in a ready position the player begins to take his racket back to his left.

He is about to play a topspin backhand drive and he steps across with his right foot.

bending the knees, and not simply dropping the head of the racket. The ball is still hit between knee- and waist-height, so the racket will be sweeping upwards on contact. Despite this, the strings should contact the back of the ball, not the bottom. The racket face should be at right angles to the ground with the inside of your wrist, facing the net. Immediately contact has been made, the wrist should start turning, so that by the time the ball has left the strings, the inside of the wrist will be facing the ground. This wrist movement will carry the racket head up the back, and over the top of the ball. The follow-through is high and across the body, with the racket finishing across your left shoulder, its head pointing to the back of the court.

Most of your early attempts at hitting topspin strokes will end up in the net. You will have to remember that the effect of topspin on a ball is to drag it down to the ground and you must aim high above the net to counter this action.

As with the forehand strokes, hitting spin on the backhand side requires only a few simple alterations

to the flat stroke you have already learned. Use an eastern backhand grip and step diagonally across with your right foot in exactly the same way you have been doing for your flat backhand. As with the forehand, spin is achieved by varying the backswing and follow-through and the action of the wrist on impact.

For a topspin backhand take the racket across the left-hand side of your body. Your racket hand should be hip-high, the racket head should be between waist- and shoulder-high and pointing towards the back of the court. As the ball approaches, step with your right foot and swing the racket head low to the ground. The racket head should be sweeping upwards as it makes contact with the back of the ball. On impact the inside of your wrist will be angled towards the ground, but should immediately begin to rotate. The inside of the wrist will be pointing to the back of the court as the ball leaves the strings, and will be angled towards the sky at the end of the follow-through. The racket head will finish pointing towards the back of the court with the right arm fully extended in the direction of the sky.

As he swings to meet the ball, the head of the racket   drops low to the ground.

The racket head is moving up as it makes contact   with the back of the ball.

Slice groundstrokes

Hitting pure underspin on a forehand drive would be counter-productive. The ball would be slow through the air and its bounce would be gentle, making an easy target for your opponent. Furthermore, to prevent the ball drifting away over the baseline, it would have to be hit low to the net, making it a high-risk shot. But, developing a sliced forehand drive, which combines a bit of underspin with a bit of sidespin, is a more sensible alternative.

Again, the sliced forehand is a variation of the flat forehand drive. The grip remains the same, the feet move in exactly the same way and the ball is still hit between knee- and waist-high. The first major difference is that the backswing for a sliced stroke is much shorter. Take the racket back so that the face is about head-high and about 30 cm (12 in) behind the line of your shoulders. Your elbow should be bent at about 90 degrees. Step across with your left foot moving the head of the racket in a gentle curve towards the ball. The strings should make contact with the back of the ball with the inside of the wrist directed towards the net. On impact the wrist should start to rotate, so that by the time the ball leaves the strings, the inside of the wrist will face the sky. The racket will finish pointing directly across the net, with your arm extended and the inside wrist still facing the sky.

Sliced strokes should be aimed low over the net to be effective. They will curve through the air and veer away low to the ground after bouncing.

For the sliced backhand drive take the racket back over your left shoulder with the racket head aimed to the back of the court. Your elbow should be bent and pointing to the net. As the ball approaches, step across with your right leg moving the racket in a shallow curve to the ball. The racket face should be at right angles to the court on impact and the inside of your wrist will be directed to the back of the court. The swing of the racket head to the ball is achieved simply by straightening your elbow. The arm should be fully extended on impact. As the racket face meets the ball, the wrist should start rotating downwards, so that as the ball leaves the strings, the inside of the wrist will be directed towards the ground. The rotation of the wrist will bring the strings down the back of the ball and across the bottom. The racket finishes pointing toward the net with the arm fully extended. The inside of the wrist is angled towards the ground.

It is worth noting that the arm, from the elbow to the shoulder, hardly moves during the sliced backhand. The movement from the backswing position to the ball is achieved by straightening the arm, and the movement of the follow-through is achieved when the left foot swings round after impact bringing the shoulders from a position sideways to the net to a position square to the net.

From his position of readiness the player starts to take his racket back to the left of his body and begins swivelling on his feet.

He has decided to play a sliced backhand stroke so he takes the racket back across his left shoulder. At the same time he steps across with his right foot.

For the sliced forehand the player takes the racket back behind his right shoulder. His elbow is bent at about 90°, his body sideways to the net.

As the player turns sideways to the net his elbow is sharply bent and the racket head is aimed at the back of the court.

At the end of the follow-through the racket will be about head-high and pointing to the net. The player's arm will be extended.

For the sliced backhand the racket will start at about shoulder-height and finish about waist-height. The player's wrist is directed to the ground.

The topspin service

One of the most obvious uses of topspin is for serving. A player who has missed his first service is naturally anxious that his second serve does not end up in the net. He wants to hit the ball high over the net, but realizes that if he hits it high and hard, it will land outside the service box. If he hits it high, but soft enough to land it in the service box, it will be easy for his opponent to make a winning return. By hitting topspin on his second service, a player can hit the ball high over the net and hard, and be confident that it will land in the service box. Furthermore, the ball will curve through the air and kick up on landing, making it doubly hard for his opponent to return.

The idea of hitting topspin on a service may sound rather complicated. After all, when hitting a serve, the ball is high in the air. How is it possible to hit *over* a ball that is above your head? Fortunately, hitting topspin on a service is easier than it sounds and can be accomplished with only a few changes to the normal service action.

For a topspin service many players prefer to use the eastern backhand grip, although it is possible to hit a perfectly adequate topspin serve with the

continental grip. The most important difference between a flat service and a spin service is in the position of the throw-up. You will remember that when hitting a flat service, the throw-up is in front of you, so that if the ball were allowed to land, it would bounce just in front of your leading foot. For the topspin service the ball should be thrown up behind you—if the ball were allowed to land it would drop behind your left heel.

The other important difference between the topspin service and the flat service is the direction in which you throw the racket head at the ball. When learning the flat service, you were told to throw the racket at the ball with the same action that you would use if you were trying to throw the racket across the net. When hitting a topspin service, you should throw the racket as if you were trying to throw it over a fence on the right-hand side of the court.

Because you are throwing the ball up behind the line of your body when serving topspin, you will have to arch your back slightly to reach it. The strings of the racket should make contact with the back of the ball and move up the back and across the top of the ball. The follow-through for this service is the same as for the flat version, with the racket arm swinging down across the body and finishing alongside the left leg.

When attempting a topspin service the player places his feet as for a flat service.

The player throws the ball up behind his left shoulder and must arch his back.

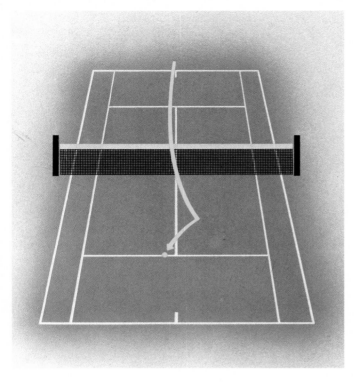

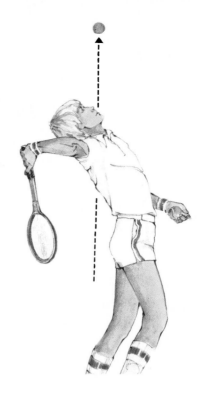

The effect of hitting topspin on a service will be to make the ball curve through the air from right to left. The ball will pass high over the net, come to earth sharply and kick up high to the right.

The movement of the racket arm is the same for a topspin service as for the flat service until the racket reaches the backscratcher position. The way the racket is 'thrown' at the ball is different.

The most important variation when hitting a topspin service is the way the ball is thrown up.

The player aims to make contact with the back of the ball while the racket head is moving upwards.

Unlike the throw-up for the flat service, the ball is thrown up a little behind the player.

The racket strings will brush up the back and over the top of the ball inducing the topspin.

The slice service

A sliced service cannot be hit high over the net and is, therefore, not a wise alternative as a second service. However, if served with slice, a ball will curve through the air and on bouncing will veer sharply away continuing in the direction of its flight path. As such, it is a very difficult ball to return and should be considered as an alternative to a flat first service.

Again, the sliced service requires only a slight variation in technique from the full flat service. As with the topspin service, the main differences are in the position of throw-up and the angle the racket is thrown at the ball.

The throw-up for a sliced service is about 30 cm (12 in) to the right of the throw-up for a flat service. If the ball were allowed to drop, it would land about 30 cm (12 in) in front of the right shoe. The racket head is thrown at an angle half way between that for the flat service and that for the topspin service.

The racket face first contacts the back of the ball with the inside of the wrist directed towards the net. On impact the wrist turns to face the left-hand side

The moment of impact. The racket moves from left to right and slightly over the top of the ball.

of the court. This action takes the face of the racket across the back of the ball and round its right side. As with the other two services, the follow-through is across the body and down the left side.

When attempting a sliced service the player positions his feet as he would for an ordinary flat service. The racket head is pointing in the direction he will hit the ball.

The player throws the ball up in the air with his left hand. Although the ball is in front of the player it is further to his right than for a normal service.

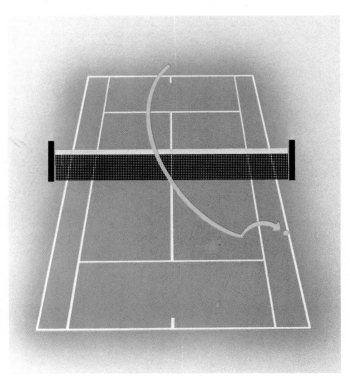

A sliced service is hit with a combination of sidespin and topspin. It will curve through the air from right to left. On bouncing it will stay low and skid off the court in the same direction as it was travelling.

For the sliced service the direction of the racket throw is to the right-hand side of the court and not directly across the net as it would be when hitting the flat service.

The position of the throw-up is an important difference between the flat service and the sliced service. For the sliced service the ball is thrown up in front and to the right of the player.

The racket follows through in the same way as it would for the flat service, down and across the left-hand side of the player's body with its head pointing towards the back of the court.

The topspin lob and drop shot

The two strokes which best illustrate the use of spin in tennis are the topspin lob and the drop shot. In the first case the ball is hit over the opponent's head, and to make sure he doesn't run back and get his racket to it after it has bounced, the topspin ensures that the ball shoots away quickly on bouncing.

The use of spin for the drop shot is aimed at achieving exactly the opposite effect. The idea with a drop shot is to catch your opponent stranded at the back of the court by just dropping the ball over the net. This shot should be hit with underspin, so that when the ball touches the ground on the far side of the net, it will hardly bounce at all, or even bounce back in the direction of the net.

You will remember that the lob is a variation of your basic drive shots on forehand and backhand. The most obvious difference is that the racket head drops much lower when hitting lobs, making contact with the underneath of the ball. The follow-through is almost straight up in the air. On impact with the ball the inside of your wrist should be directed towards the sky.

For the topspin lob the racket head must drop low to the ground as it swings to meet the ball. But the point of contact should be the back of the ball, not the underneath. The inside of the wrist should be directed to the net on impact, and the strings of the racket should sweep sharply up the back of the

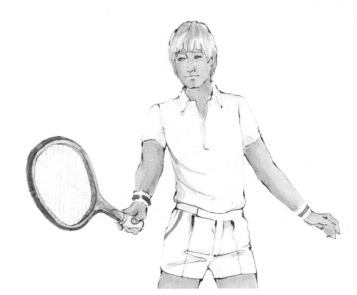

The wrist action for a drop shot: as the racket face meets the back of the ball the player's wrist is directed down towards the court.

ball. The follow-through is almost vertical through the air, with the racket finishing above the right shoulder, its head pointing to the back of the court.

The topspin lob requires a considerable amount of skill. The ball will not reach the same height as the flat lob, and will dip sharply towards the court on its journey through the air.

Most experienced tennis players would agree that the stroke requiring the greatest amount of skill in its execution and timing is the drop shot. The drop shot relies on an element of surprise to achieve its effect. If your opponent is aware of your intentions when trying this stroke, it will rarely succeed.

When hitting a topspin lob the player takes his racket back a little further than for a flat lob. He drops the racket head low to the ground as he swings to meet the ball.

The follow-through is almost vertical. The racket head finishes high above the player's head but on the same side of his body as he played the ball.

The player starts to rotate his wrist. The strings of the racket move down and under the back of the ball.

The player will continue to rotate his wrist even after the ball has left the strings. The inside of the wrist should be directed up in the air.

Disguise, therefore, is an important ingredient when attempting to drop shot your opponent. A good drop shot should clear the net by not more than 60 cm (2 ft) and land within about a metre (3 ft) of the net. It is important that the ball should not bounce too high in the direction of your opponent. If struck correctly, the ball should 'die' on touching the opponent's half of the court, or even bounce back towards the net.

Line up for the forehand drop shot as you would for a forehand drive, holding the racket with an eastern backhand grip. The backswing and footwork stay the same but the swing towards the ball should be gentle and the ball should be hit closer to the body with the elbow slightly bent on impact. The racket face should meet the back of the ball, with the inside of the wrist directed towards the net. On contact, the wrist should rotate sharply so the inside of the wrist is facing the sky, and the follow-through should be almost vertical up in the air. The racket finishes in front of the player, its head pointing to the sky. The racket hand should be about head-high with the inside of the wrist directed towards the player's face.

The further back you stand, the harder it is to play this stroke successfully. It is rarely advisable to attempt a drop shot from behind the service line.

The drop shot: the player takes his racket back as for a forehand drive, but using an eastern backhand grip.

The player twists the racket so that the strings pass underneath the ball. This movement will impart backspin to the ball.

The follow-through is short. The player's elbow is bent on impact with the ball, and at the end of the follow-through.

8 The history of the game

The early days

Tennis, or lawn tennis to give it its proper name, was born in Victorian Britain. People wanted a game that was more active than croquet and that could be played on the lawns of a country house. It was made possible by a technical advance—the development of an indiarubber ball—and the growth of the game was largely due to the commercial spirit of a former major in the Indian army, a certain Walter Clopton Wingfield.

In the latter part of the nineteenth century, with the British Empire at its height, the growing middle classes were looking for new ways of spending their increasing leisure time. Weekend garden parties were all the rage and croquet had become a popular pastime at these social gatherings. But there were those who longed for a more active way of passing the long summer afternoons.

This photograph of an early tennis match emphasizes the social aspect of the game which became popular in Victorian England. This photograph was taken in 1878 by which time the rectangular court was used.

A ladies' doubles match in the 1880s. The ankle-length dresses had to be hitched up with one hand when a ball was pursued. Bustles, corsets, high necks and hats could not have aided mobility.

Cricket was the established summer sport in Britain at the time, but it was hardly a suitable game for the confines of a garden lawn. More important, perhaps, the hard ball used to play cricket would have been thought dangerous in mixed company. Any new game would have to allow members of both sexes the opportunity to meet and mingle—match-making was an important side issue at these Victorian get-togethers.

Games involving rackets and balls had long been in existence. Chief among these were rackets and real tennis. Curiously, the game of rackets had begun life in a debtor's prison near London's Fleet Street, probably about the end of the eighteenth century. The balls were almost certainly made out of leather, and the rackets crudely fashioned from wood. The game of rackets, which is rather similar to modern-day squash, became a popular way for the men to ease the monotony of prison life, making the best use of the facilities—stone walls and floors.

The game that was to be the other main inspiration for lawn tennis had a rather nobler ancestry. Real, or royal tennis, was a popular pastime of Henry VIII. The courts where the king used to play are still in existence at Hampton Court and can be visited by members of the public. Henry had borrowed the game from France where it was popular with the

French monarchs as early as the fourteenth century.

Real tennis is played in a long, stone-flagged hall. A net is draped across the centre and galleries, in which spectators can sit, run the length of the court on each side. The players stand at each end of the hall and hit the ball backwards and forwards across the net. The game is different in many ways to the tennis we are familiar with today—the ball can be bounced off the walls or rolled along the roof of the galleries. The rules are extremely complicated, but the similarities between this game and the one we know today as tennis are obvious.

Returning to our Victorian garden party with all those sporting types hitting croquet balls about the place and getting frightfully bored, relief was close at hand with the development of a ball made from rubber. There had been various experiments to adapt games using rackets and balls for outdoor use, but the balls used in rackets and real tennis would not bounce on grass.

In 1872 a man called Harry Gem wrote about a game he had devised which was like real tennis but could be played outdoors on grass with balls specially made from rubber. However, it was Major Walter Wingfield who took the development of this new outdoor game a stage further. Realizing the commercial possibilities of a game that could be played as an alternative to croquet, Wingfield drew up a set of rules, designed a court, christened his brain-child Spharistiké—a Greek word meaning ball game—and set off for the Patents Office.

Spharistiké was soon on sale in the shops of Victorian Britain. A box containing two rackets, balls, a net, white tape for marking the court, net posts and assorted skewers, could be bought for five guineas. Sales boomed.

Wingfield's game quickly became very popular, but it was still to undergo many changes before it developed into the game we play today. The court, for example, was a rather strange shape, narrowing at the net and widening out at the two baselines. The court markings bore little resemblance to the ones we are familiar with on tennis courts today. The net, too, was a different shape, and the scoring system was borrowed from the game of rackets and would be more familiar to a modern-day squash player than a tennis player. Still, it was a beginning, and many would say *the* beginning.

At about this time the editor of *The Field* magazine was a keen sportsman called J. W. Walsh. His assistant, equally enthusiastic about games of all types, was a man called Henry Jones. Walsh was one of the garden-party set. The parties he held in the large grounds of his London house were very popular, but unfortunately his flower beds were being trampled by his croquet-playing friends. To solve this problem, Jones was sent out to find a suitable plot of land in the London area where a croquet club could be founded.

Alarmed at the high rents being asked for land in the central, select areas of London, Jones ventured further afield, finally coming upon a suitable plot by Worple Road, in one of London's less fashionable suburbs, Wimbledon. In 1870 the All England Croquet Club was founded and, for a time, flourished. But by 1875 the club's fortunes were floundering, membership had dwindled and there was difficulty in paying the rent.

Walsh and Jones had closely followed the growth of the game of tennis, and particularly the development of the tennis ball. In 1874 a man called Heathcote wrote to *The Field* about the improved playing properties of a tennis ball he had designed. Heathcote's ball, although rubber, was stitched around with cloth. The new ball, it was claimed, considerably increased the amount of control a player could achieve, and added a new dimension of skill to the game of lawn tennis. The letter stirred the imagination of our sporting duo and indicated to them the direction their croquet club should take. In 1875 lawn tennis and badminton were introduced into the club's activities; in 1877 the club's name was changed to include the

This early illustration of a game of tennis shows the type of court patented by Major Walter Clopton Wingfield. Note the hour-glass shape of the court.

Women started playing at the Wimbledon Championships in 1884. This picture of a women's tennis match at Worple Road, before the Championships moved to Church Road, was taken in 1900.

word 'Tennis', and that year a tournament was held.

From 1875, when Wingfield first introduced his new game, to 1877 there were few developments. The game was known as 'Sticky' by those Victorians who found the Greek original too much of a mouthful before the name lawn tennis was adopted. The Marylebone Cricket Club, the MCC, set itself up as the governing body for the game, as it was for cricket, croquet and real tennis, and a few minor adjustments were made to the rules. But when Jones and Walsh decided to hold a tournament, they looked long and hard at Wingfield's rule book and made many fundamental alterations.

The shape of the court was changed to the one we are familiar with today. The net was lowered and the real tennis scoring system was adopted in preference to the racket system which had been used up until then. The championships were scheduled to begin on Monday, 9 July 1877 and to continue until they were completed. No play would take place on the Friday and Saturday of that week so as not to conflict with the Eton v Harrow cricket match—a prominent event in the social calendar of Victorian England.

The first Wimbledon final took place on 19 July, having been delayed somewhat by rain. The finalists were a 26-year-old Wimbledon resident called Spencer Gore and a former Cambridge Blue called William Marshall. Two hundred spectators turned up at the Worple Road ground on a wet and blustery day. In the event Spencer Gore, a rackets player of considerable standing, beat William Marshall, a renowned real tennis player, 6–2, 6–5, 6–2. It was to be the start of something big.

The growth of the game

One wonders what Spencer Gore would think if he could be transported through time to a modern-day Wimbledon Championships. Probably the first thing

he would notice would be that the tournament has moved from its original location to a site to the north of the first championships.

Lawn tennis grew in popularity during the early years of the twentieth century, and in 1913 improvements were made to the facilities at Worple Road, increasing the seating from 2,000 to 3,200. During the course of World War I the tournament did not take place, but when the championships resumed in 1919, it was clear that the All England Club would have to find a new and larger home. In 1920 an architect was employed to design a club house for a plot of land that had been bought in nearby Church Road, and in 1922 the championships were held for the first time at their present address.

Gore would almost certainly be amazed by the crowds that flock to see Wimbledon each year. Only 200 spectators turned up to watch him win the first Wimbledon final back in 1877. The present Wimbledon Centre Court holds 15,000 spectators and is invariably full throughout the course of the championships. But even the crowds that pack the Centre Court each year are dwarfed by the milling throng that

Blanche Hillyard was a great lady player of her day. She won the Wimbledon Championship in 1886, 1889, 1894, 1897, 1899, and 1900. This picture, taken in 1900 illustrates what lady players of the day wore on court.

Bunny Austin caused a revolution in tennis wear for men when he played at the 1933 Wimbledon Championships wearing shorts.

follows the tournament on the outside courts. About 300,000 spectators visit Wimbledon each year.

Once our 1877 champion had elbowed his way through the crush, he would be in for quite a shock. By Victorian standards the clothes worn by today's tennis players are quite indecent. A reason often put forward for the quick growth of tennis in Victorian times was that it gave the men of the day a chance to glimpse a lady's ankle as she pursued the ball across the lawn! In those days a man would go on court wearing long trousers, sometimes tucked into knee-length stockings, a loose-fitting shirt, and possibly a waistcoat or blazer, a tie and a hat. His shoes would have been made from leather with flat-bottomed soles. Lady players of the day—it was not until 1884 that women competed at Wimbledon—would have worn ground-length summer dresses with high collars, pinched waists, bustles, tightly-laced corsets and hats.

All-white outfits for tennis became fashionable towards the end of the nineteenth century, and it was stipulated by the All England Club that only 'whites' could be worn on court. This convention was also accepted by many of the tennis clubs that were springing up all over Britain and in other countries. Long trousers remained the dress requirement for men until 1934 when Bunny Austin, a leading British player of the day, appeared wearing shorts. At first it was thought in his hurry to get to the court, that he had forgotten his trousers, but once people realized that this fashion was very much more sensible, most male players quickly followed suit and long trousers became a thing of the past.

My Partner

Above A postcard of *c.* 1910. *Below* A magazine cover of World War I.

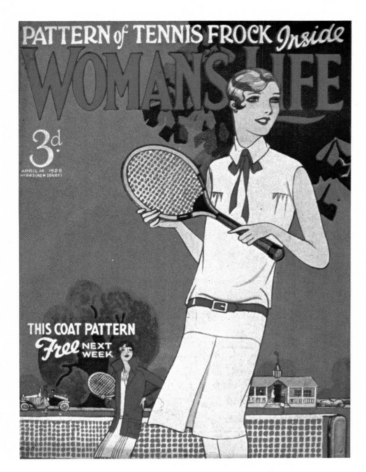

PATTERN of TENNIS FROCK Inside
WOMANS LIFE
3d.
APRIL 14 1928
N°843(NEW SERIES)
THIS COAT PATTERN Free NEXT WEEK

The revolution in women's tennis wear had begun fifteen years before Austin arrived in shorts. Although the flamboyant tennis outfits of the early days were soon abandoned in favour of more sober and practical costumes, women's tennis dresses remained ankle-length up until World War I. Of course, bustles were no longer worn, hats were optional and elaborate petticoats were dispensed with. Still, necklines remained high, restricting movement of the head, and pinched waists with all the accompanying corsetry remained. The wind of change in women's tennis wear was to blow from France.

In 1919 Suzanne Lenglen, a French girl who was destined to become a legendary figure in lawn tennis, turned up at Wimbledon wearing a flimsy, one-piece cotton frock. The hemline was just below the knee, and those restricting corsets that had persisted for so long were abandoned. The effect on tennis was electric. Lenglen soon achieved superstar status, admired by the women and adored by the men. Not until thirty years later did a fashion innovation cause such a sensation as Lenglen's 1919 Wimbledon outfit. The year was 1949, the player was Gussie Moran, the innovation—frilly knickers!

Teddy Tinling's first experience of Wimbledon was as a ballboy. He was to become a doubles player of some note, but it is not for his tennis that Tinling will be remembered. Besides ballboying and competing at Wimbledon, Tinling was also an umpire and had the job of checking that the players were correctly dressed before escorting them to the court.

Below Suzanne Lenglen was not only the leading woman player of her day but her stylish outfits set the trend in tennis wear.

Above The trend in shorter dresses was soon highlighted in the fashionable magazines.

His artistic temperament and interest in tennis fashion launched Tinling on a career as a tennis couturier. By the late 1940s he was designing many of the outfits for the leading lady players of the day. No doubt he will best be remembered as the man who brought frills to Wimbledon, but he remains today the foremost designer of women's tennis outfits.

By contrast with many of the things he would see around him, Gore would find the equipment used by today's players quite familiar. Balls have changed little in the last hundred years. Rackets, although available in materials other than wood, are essentially the same as the one used by Gore in that first Wimbledon final. On court the net would have been a little higher, but the court markings and scoring system have remained virtually unchanged.

I suspect it would be the tactics and technique of today's players that would interest Gore most. Reports of the first Wimbledon Championships attribute Gore's success to his tactic of coming up to the net at every opportunity and returning his opponent's shot before it had time to bounce. This technique is called 'volleying' and is still considered the most successful method of play on fast courts. The overhead service would, no doubt, interest our Victorian interloper—in his day the ball was put into

1949 saw the introduction of a new fashion for ladies when little-known American Gussie Moran appeared at Wimbledon wearing frilly knickers. The crowds were shocked and the new fashion was in every newspaper the next day.

play underarm or at shoulder-height—and the top-spin techniques of players like Bjorn Borg and Guillermo Vilas would be a revelation.

The recent past

In the early days of lawn tennis the Marylebone Cricket Club set itself up as the official governing body for the new game. At the time the pioneers of tennis were flattered that such an established body should take an interest in their baby. But as the game grew, tennis players felt they should have more control over their own affairs. When the All England Club rewrote the rule book in 1877, it was agreed by all concerned that the club should take over from the MCC. The All England Club continued its function as the governing body for the game until 1888, when the Lawn Tennis Association, the present administrators of the game, was formed.

Considering the limitations of travel and communications in the nineteenth century, the new game crossed the seas surprisingly rapidly. There is a record of a tennis tournament taking place at Nahant, Massachusets in 1876. The same year the New Orleans Lawn Tennis Club was formed, and in 1881 the United States Lawn Tennis Association was founded to look after the game in America.

As the game spread throughout the world, the individual countries where it was played formed their own national associations. These associations adopted the rules published by the All England Club and

This 1920s poster produced by the French motor company Citroën illustrates how fashionable tennis had become in France.

LA **CITROEN** ET TOUS LES SPORTS

LE TENNIS

Above This photograph of an early game of lawn tennis in America was taken in 1880.

Below Here American players enjoy the sunshine in New York's Central Park. The picture is dated 1896.

Besides the honour of winning what is still the world's most prestigious tennis tournament and a miniature replica of the trophy which he can keep, a modern Wimbledon Champion gets a very sizeable cheque. When Gore won the tournament in 1877, he was presented with a cup valued at 25 gns which he had to return at the end of the year. When Bjorn Borg won a hundred years later, his little envelope contained a cheque for £15,000.

In Gore's day tennis was merely a recreation—a game played purely for enjoyment and the honour of winning this or that tournament. There certainly would have been no opportunity for a player to win prize money, and indeed most of those early players would probably not have needed it. If a player was down on his luck and had to supplement his income by teaching the game, he would not have been allowed to enter into a tournament and would probably have been barred from membership of a club.

looked on the British authorities as the governing body for the game world-wide. This remained the situation until 1913, when it was considered improper that one country, albeit the parent country, should monopolize the control of such an international sport. The International Lawn Tennis Federation was formed with thirteen member nations, and this organization took over many of the responsibilities of the British Lawn Tennis Association. Today the Federation has dropped the word 'Lawn' from its title, has more than a hundred member nations and remains the international controlling body for the sport.

It is quite possible that Spencer Gore would not even notice one of the most fundamental changes that have occurred since his day. He might get a clue if he were to watch very closely the presentation ceremony at the end of the Wimbledon Championships. The winner is handed a magnificent trophy . . . and an envelope. Were he even to notice the envelope, it is unlikely that he would guess its contents.

Donald Budge is believed by many to be the best male tennis player of all times. Budge is best known for his method of hitting a backhand—his was possibly the first topspin backhand used in top-class tennis.

William Tatem Tilden was one of the giants of tennis in every way. Born in Philadelphia in 1893 and nicknamed Big Bill,

Tilden towered over his opponents. He won Wimbledon in 1920 and 1921 then again in 1930 at the age of 37.

Until about ten years ago the public image of tennis was a game played by amateurs for enjoyment— certainly not for money. But as long ago as the 1920s the seeds for change were being sown. It was about this time that an American businessman called C.C. (Cash and Carry) Pyle realized that tennis could attract big crowds. Pyle signed up some of the top amateur players of the day, including the legendary Miss Lenglen, and organized a nationwide tour of the United States. The tour opened at New York's Madison Square Gardens, where takings were more than $40,000. The tour was a great success, and between then and World War II a number of similar tours were organized and the list of amateur players turning professional grew.

One of the first touring professional players giving exhibition matches throughout the States was the American who dominated Wimbledon in 1920 and 1921, William (Big Bill) Tilden. The Czech Karel Kozeluh and the American Vincent Richards joined Tilden on his early tours and later the German Hans Nusslein toured with Tilden in the early 30s. Ellsworth Vines, Fred Perry and Donald Budge were some of the other great names to join the professional tours in the 30s. In the 40s Bobby Riggs, Donald Budge and Jack Kramer, all great names in their amateur days, signed up as professionals. This switch from the amateur ranks to the professionals continued throughout the 50s and 60s, and included Trabert,

Rosewall, Hoad, Gimeno, Olmedo, Buchholz and Laver. Then in 1967 an oil millionaire and sports fanatic called Lamar Hunt teamed up with a struggling tennis promoter called Dave Dixon and formed a company called World Championship Tennis.

Hunt's effect on tennis in the mid-60s can be compared with the impact of Kerry Packer on cricket in recent years. Money was no object to the Texas oilman and he set about signing up all the top amateurs of the day, including John Newcombe, Tony Roche, Cliff Drysdale, Nikki Pilic and Roger Taylor. Amateur tennis could stand the occasional loss of one of its star players but the events of 1967 were too much.

To try to prevent top amateur names turning professional it had become the practice for tournament organizers to make under-the-counter payments to amateurs playing in their tournaments. How widespread this practice had become and how long it had been going on for is not clear, but it was generally disliked by many of the administrators of the amateur game. One such administrator, Herman David, who was Chairman of the All England Club in the mid-60s, decided that the time had come to end distinctions between amateurs and professionals. In 1967 he announced that the rest of the world could do as they please, but in future Wimbledon would be open to amateurs and professionals alike. The rest of the world quickly followed on Wimbledon's heels.

The first 'open' Wimbledon took place in 1968. Rod Laver won the men's singles and collected a cheque for £2,000. The ladies' winner was Billie Jean King, whose prize money was £750.

Sweden's Bjorn Borg holds high the trophy he won at the centenary Wimbledon Championships in 1977. He first won the Championship in 1976 and was to make it four-in-a-row by winning in 1979

9 The language of tennis

Tennis, like most sports or specialist activities, has a language all its own. This doesn't mean that you will need to take a tennis phrase book along with you when you go to buy a racket, or need an interpreter when talking to a tennis coach. But there are a number of terms and expressions which are peculiar to tennis and you may not always understand their meaning unless these have been explained to you.

The terminology of tennis can be divided into three basic categories, although their borders will not always be clearly defined. There is the official rule-book language—the words used to describe the system of scoring, the layout of the court and the procedures of play. The language of the rule book is very formal, like a legal document. The rules were written at the end of the nineteenth century, so their language has a strong Victorian flavour. But because so much of tennis was borrowed from earlier games, many of the words used date back to the reigns of monarchs much earlier than Queen Victoria.

There is also the language of the tennis instructor. Much of this will be concerned with the techniques, tactics and training involved in playing tennis. A tennis coach will, of course, depend on the language of the rule book when explaining the regulations of the game, but he will need to supplement his official vocabulary with many new phrases to describe the way tennis is actually played.

Then there is the language of the players. This is tennis-court slang—the words and expressions used by the players to communicate between themselves. This language will differ from country to country and even from region to region, although certain phrases used by tennis players are international. Into this category comes the phraseology of the professionals. Because the majority of full-time tennis players are American, the language of most top tennis stars is rich with campus slang. Even British players, once they start 'playing the circuit', acquire a strong American accent before long.

The report you read in a newspaper, or the commentary you hear on the radio or television, will be based largely on the language of the rule book and the tennis instructor—some of the expressions used by tennis players would be too obscure for a widely based audience, many of whom don't even play the game of tennis. Where a broadcaster uses an expression that might not be familiar, he will usually take a

The umpire is in charge of officiating at a tennis match. He is usually seated on a special high chair beside the court and adjacent to the net.

little time to explain what it means, although when a player is interviewed, it can be useful to know some of the common jargon used by the professional players.

Much of the official language of tennis is common sense. Even someone who had never seen a tennis court in his life before would probably be able to guess the names of many of the lines—the location of the baseline, sidelines and centrelines can be easily deduced, although you would have to know a little about the game to pin-point the position of the service line. Anyone who didn't know might think it is the line behind which you serve, whereas this is in fact the baseline.

Some of the official terminology of tennis is less easily explained. Its origin dates back many hundreds of years and its derivation can only be guessed at. The word tennis is an example. The name was taken from real or royal tennis, a racket game played by Henry VIII. But just what does the word tennis mean? We know that Henry borrowed the game from the French, but the French name was *Jeu de Paulme*—when it was first played in France, the ball was hit with the palm of the hand. A popular explanation is that tennis comes from the French word *tenez*—to you—and that the early players used to shout out the word when hitting the ball over the net. But this is speculation, as is the theory for the origin of the word 'love'. When lawn tennis was started, the scoring system was taken from the game of rackets, but when the rules were changed for the first Wimbledon, the real-tennis system was adopted. So the word love was probably used by Henry VIII when playing the game at Hampton Court. A popular explanation is that it comes from the French word *l'oeuf*, meaning an egg. In cricket the term duck is used when a player scores no runs. That is because the original phrase was 'out for a duck's egg'. A duck's egg is round in shape and looks like a nought.

It is thought that the word 'service' dates back to the early days of real tennis, when the ball was put in play by a servant. The term 'deuce', when the score is at 40-all, comes from the French word for two— *deux*—for the player who wins two consecutive points wins the game. The term 'advantage', when a player having been at deuce has won the next point and needs to gain one more point to take the game, is self-evident.

The language of the tennis coach is a sort of tennis trade talk. Of course, many of the phrases he uses will be technical—terms that have been originated to describe methods of playing the game and the equipment that a tennis player uses. He will use the formal language of the coaching manuals, as well as the jargon he has developed to communicate more easily

Through the medium of television, the Wimbledon Championships are seen live in more than 15 countries and many more countries show recorded film of the event.

with his pupils. Expressions like 'chopper' for the continental grip, 'shakehands' for the eastern forehand grip, are common coaching slang the word over. 'The pendulum swing' and 'the backscratcher', are also terms used by coaches wherever tennis is taught, and there are many more expressions, some international in their use and some of more local significance.

Of course, the language of the coach changes gradually over the years. New techniques of play become fashionable and words are invented to describe them. Certain styles become obsolete and the terms used to describe them disappear from common usage.

The jargon used by the professional players is of a far more transitory nature. It is a sort of verbal shorthand—a way of communicating vividly in the high-speed world of international sport. Their conversation concerns itself with the pressures of playing top-class tennis. The 'pros' talk about 'the circuit' or 'the tour', and they are concerned with their 'ranking'. A player who is not trying to win for one reason or other is said to be 'tanking'; a player who becomes too nervous and lets victory slip away is said to have 'choked' or got 'the elbow'. More familiar expressions become abbreviated or shortened in the mouths of the full-time tennis players. A player who has won a game on the other player's service—not having lost his own service—is said to have the 'break'.

The language of the ordinary tennis player, the person who plays at a club or in the park, will also contain terms that are not in the rule book, or coaching manuals. Some will include terms used only in the particular country or region in which he plays, although many of his expressions will be understood world-wide. The terms 'rough' and 'smooth' when a racket is 'spun' or 'tossed' for service or 'ends' are fairly international, but the way in which a player calls the score during a game may vary from place to place. For fifteen, some players say five—instead of fifteen-all they will call the score as five-all. The way in which some players call the advantage score can also differ. In Britain it is common to say van-in when the server has the advantage, and van-out when it is the receiver's advantage. Americans generally refer to the score as ad-in and ad-out respectively.

I have concentrated on the universal language of tennis. As your experience grows you will almost certainly come across expressions not mentioned in this book, tennis talk with a local flavour. When you are faced with a word or expression you have not heard before, discover its meaning—it could be a useful addition to your tennis vocabulary.

It is possible to survive in most countries without knowing the language . . . but if you want more than just to survive, it is worth learning the lingo.

Glossary of tennis terms

Ace   A service winner when the receiver does not touch the ball.
Ad-in   American term for the score following deuce when it is the server's advantage.
Ad-out   American term for the score following deuce when it is the receiver's advantage.
Advantage   The player winning a point after deuce is said to have the advantage.
Alley   American term for singles and doubles sidelines.

Backhand   Stroke for playing a ball that comes to a player on the opposite side to that on which he holds his racket.
Backscratcher   Racket movement during service when the racket head is taken over the shoulder and drops down the player's back.
Ball   Pressurized rubber ball stitched around with cloth, the weight and dimensions of which are defined in rule 3.
Break point   Point which if won by the receiver will give him the game.

Change over   Period of time allocated for players to change ends.
Chopper grip   *See* Continental grip.
Closed tournament   Tournament where entry is restricted to certain categories of player—national, local, amateur and so on.
Continental grip   Sometimes called the chopper grip because the racket is held in the same way as you would hold a chopper when cutting firewood. Popular grip for serving and volleying (*see page 22*).
Court   The area marked out for playing tennis.
Court markings   These are the baselines, sidelines, service lines, centre lines and centre marks.
Court officials   These include the umpire, line-judges, foot-fault judge, net-cord judge, ballboys or ballgirls.
Court surfaces   Types of court, principally grass, shale (clay) and hard.
Cross-court   An angled return.

Deuce   The score in a game when both players have won three points each—40 all.

Doubles   Game of tennis involving four players.
Double fault   Fault on consecutive first and second serves.
Down-the-line   A return parallel with and close to the sideline.
Draw   Method of deciding who plays whom in the first round of a tournament.
Drop shot   Stroke whereby the ball is played gently over the net with back spin, and used when the opponent is at the back of the court.

Eastern grip   Most common grip for hitting groundstrokes, sometimes called the shakehands grip. *See page 16* for the eastern forehand grip, *page 18* for the eastern backhand grip, and *page 20* for the double eastern grip.

Fault   An illegal service or return resulting in a point awarded to the opponent, unless the fault is on a first service, in which case a second service is allowed.
Five   Term sometimes used instead of 15 when calling the score.
Foot-fault   Fault made during service by the server touching the baseline before hitting the ball, touching the foot down in the court before hitting the ball, or running or walking during the course of the service. The server's feet must be behind the baseline between the centre mark and sideline.
Forehand   Stroke for playing a ball that comes to the side of a player's body on which he holds his racket.

Game   A sequence of points as specified in the rules.
Grand slam   Term for the feat of winning Wimbledon, Australian, French and US Championships in the same year.
Grips   Methods of holding the racket—principally eastern, western and continental.
Groundstroke   Method of hitting the ball after it has bounced.

In play   The status of the ball during the course of a point.

Let   An occurrence during a point which requires that the point should be replayed, such as a ball rolling across from another court or a disputed call. A service let occurs when the served ball hits the net and bounces into the correct service box.
Lob   Stroke whereby the ball is hit up in the air. Used to return balls over the head and out of reach of the opponent.
Long ball   Ball that lands over the baseline, or over the service line during a serve.
Love   The word used for nought when scoring in tennis.

Match   A sequence of sets as specified in the rules. Usually the best of three or five sets.
Mixed doubles   Doubles match in which each pair is made up of a male and a female player.

Net cord   A stroke other than a service where the ball hits the net but continues its flight across the net and lands in court.

Open tournament   Tournament open to professionals and amateurs alike.
Order of play   Document listing who plays whom and on which court, displayed at a tournament.

Pendulum swing   Racket movement during service when the racket head swings down like a pendulum past the player's leg.
Play two   Order to replay the service point starting from the first serve.
Point   A point begins when one of the players serves the ball and ends when the ball goes out of play.

Racket   Implement for hitting the ball.
Receiver   The player whose turn it is to receive service.
Rough/smooth   Terms denoting the way in which the trebling is threaded on the face of a racket.
Rubber   In team competitions a sequence of sets is called a rubber and the overall competition is called a match.

Score board   Board by the court depicting the match score.
Score sheet   Form used by the umpire for keeping the score.
Seeding   Method of segregating the best players in the early rounds of tournaments.
Serve and volley   Tacting of serving and approaching the net to volley the service return.
Server   The player whose turn it is to serve.
Service   Method of putting the ball in play at the beginning of each point.
Set   A sequence of games as specified in the rules.
Singles   Game of tennis involving two players.
Slice   Ball hit with a combination of underspin and sidespin or, when serving, a combination of topspin and sidespin.
Smash   Stroke whereby the player hits a ball that has been played to him above head-level. A smash is an overhead shot hit with power.
Spin   The way a ball rotates in flight—principally topspin, underspin, slice and sidespin.

Tie-break   Method of determining the outcome of a set when the game score is level. A number of different tie-break systems exist. Generally the player whose turn it is to serve serves one point. His opponent then serves twice, the first player then serves twice, and so on. The points are awarded in straight numerical progression. After six points have been played the players change ends. The winner of the tie-break, and therefore the winner of the set, is the person who first reaches seven points, provided he is two points ahead of his opponent.
Toss   Method of deciding which player serves first in a match.
Tramlines   British term for singles and doubles sidelines.

Van-in   British expression for the score following deuce when it is the server's advantage.
Van-out   British expression for the score following deuce when it is the receiver's advantage.
Volley   Stroke hit before the ball has bounced.

Western grip   Method of gripping the racket when hitting forehand, not often used by top-class players, the main exceptions being Bjorn Borg and Sue Barker. To find this grip, hold the racket in an eastern forehand grip and then rotate the grip hand about 1 cm ($\frac{1}{2}$ in) clockwise.
Wide ball   Ball that lands outside the sideline or to the left or right of the service box during a serve.

10 Where do I go from here?

Having reached the last chapter of this book you should now have a good idea of what the game of tennis is all about—that is if you're not one of those people who opens a book at the end and works back! You should by now know what is involved in learning how to play and you will have acquired some useful background information on the game. But where do you go from here?

Hopefully, by now, you will feel that your game is making progress. But just how good you are on a tennis court will depend largely on how much of this book you have absorbed and how much time you have devoted to practising what you have read. Remember, you can't become a good tennis player overnight. You can't become a good player in a few weeks or even a few months. It is just possible to reach a good standard of play in six months, but you would need to devote all your waking hours to practising, and even then you would require a great deal of natural ability and personal guidance from a good coach.

So, if you feel that you are making progress, however slight, it is worth persevering with the game. Once you have decided that you want to take up tennis seriously as one of your main leisure activities, you will probably want to become more involved with the game. Almost certainly you will wish to test your new-found skills against more experienced players and possibly you would like to play for a team, or enter tournaments.

At this stage in your tennis development you should start thinking about having personal lessons from a trained instructor and joining a tennis club. Both these steps will involve you in expense, and a certain amount of thought should be given before embarking on either course.

Paying for tennis lessons can be a costly business and, of course, if the expense of tennis lessons can be avoided or minimized, so much the better. Reading an instructional tennis book before seeking advice from a coach will prove of great value. Provided you have grasped the basic concepts of the game, your coach will be able to start your instruction at a more advanced stage and you will be able to cover more ground in a short time. On the other hand, don't give a coach the impression that you know it all. If you have taken the trouble to choose a qualified instructor, you should put yourself in his hands, and accept the advice that he gives.

Unless you know what to expect, your early tennis lessons may be a let down. The purpose of taking lessons is not to get out on a court and have a good playing session with a more talented player. It is unlikely that your coach will actually 'play' with you until you are much more advanced. There would be little point—he should be able to beat you easily in your early years of playing tennis—and you would gain little from the experience other than losing confidence in your own ability.

You may find that a coach suggests that you change some of your favourite strokes. You may feel that your service or volley is particularly good and you cannot see why it should be altered. Remember your coach will be far more experienced than you. Although the strokes he wants you to alter may be quite effective against your friends in the park or at school, your instructor will be looking into the future. He will want to develop your strokes so that they will be effective against the players you are likely to meet in years to come. If you are paying good money for tennis instruction, you would be foolish to reject the advice your instructor gives.

A good player doesn't necessarily make a good coach. Teaching tennis requires certain abilities that are not essential for reaching the top as a player. The ability to communicate, often with someone younger and much less knowledgeable, the ability to maintain the pupil's interest even when dealing with the basic stages of the game, and patience, are the important qualities to look for in a coach.

Below Make the best use of what your coach teaches you by practising.

Right Follow your coach's advice if he asks you to alter your style.

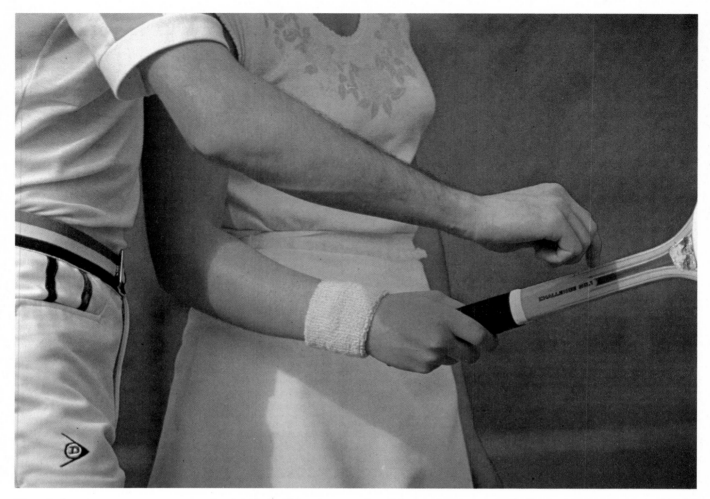

Tennis lessons are expensive so try to make sure that you find the right coach with professional qualifications. A coach will be able to advise you on tennis equipment and clubs.

Getting instruction from the right coach is obviously an important step in your development as a player. But how do you go about finding somebody suitable? Of course, a personal recommendation from a satisfied customer is by far the best way of selecting a coach. But if you do not know anyone who has had tennis instruction, this will perhaps be difficult. Your games teacher at school may know somebody suitable, or your parents could enquire among their friends and colleagues at work. Failing this, you should phone or write to your national tennis association, who will let you have a list of qualified instructors in your area.

In the absence of any other guidelines—such as personal references—it is advisable to select an instructor who has coaching qualifications. There is nothing to stop anyone from setting themselves up as a tennis coach, and while they may be excellent players in their own right, unless they have undergone the various courses and examinations run by the national associations, their ability to instruct may be limited.

Besides helping you with your technique, a coach will be able to advise you on many other points relating to the game of tennis. He will be in a good position to recommend which are the best shops in the area for buying equipment. He will almost certainly be able to guide you in your choice of equipment and may

be able to secure a small discount on your purchases. But be a little cautious: many coaches receive commission on sales to their pupils at local sports shops. Provided you have chosen your instructor well, his advice will be good. If, however, you feel that you are being asked to buy items you don't think you really need, try to get a second opinion before spending your money.

Joining a tennis club is another big step for a young tennis player. It may seem an unnecessary waste of money, particularly if you have easy access to public courts, or are lucky enough to have a tennis court in your own garden. In fact, belonging to a club is almost essential for anyone wishing to reach a good standard as a player. As a club member you will be able to meet and play against a far wider range of players, than if your tennis is restricted to playing your friends at school or in the local park. To become a good player you must practise your game against players of differing styles and standards. This is rarely possible unless you join a tennis club.

At most clubs your membership fee entitles you to unlimited use of the club's facilities. If you intend reaching a high standard by playing on public courts, the hourly hire-charge will quickly mount up. Reaching a good standard will almost certainly require that you play an average of two hours a day throughout the year and this would be far more expensive if paid at the hourly rates of most public parks than the membership fee of most clubs.

There are other advantages in belonging to a tennis

club and these will be considered later in this chapter, but first, how does one go about joining a tennis club?

Again, personal recommendation is by far the best method. If you have a friend who is already a member, he will be able to tell you about the club to which he belongs. It is also an advantage to join a club where you already know somebody, for this helps you settle in more quickly. If you are taking instruction, your coach should be able to advise you on the local clubs. Provided he has had time to assess your playing standard and get to know you as a person, he will be able to recommend the club he thinks most suitable. On the other hand, he may feel that your game has not developed sufficiently for club membership—most tennis clubs set a minimum playing standard for their members. Standards tend to vary from club to club and your coach will certainly know if you are good enough to join any of the local clubs, or whether you should develop your game a little more before making an application.

In the event that you do not know anyone who is a member of a local club, you are not taking lessons, or your coach is new to the area and not familiar with the local clubs, you will be able to get a list of clubs in your region from your national association. The list will only give the addresses and phone numbers of the clubs and possibly the names of the secretaries. You will need to know much more about the club before deciding whether to apply for membership.

A local institution such as a library will almost certainly have a list of sporting amenities in the neighbourhood, and they will probably be able to give you much more information about local tennis clubs. The sort of things you will want to know will be the size of the club—the number of members and the number of courts, the type of courts, whether there is a junior section, membership fees, and so on.

Transport consideration will almost certainly play an important part in your choice of club. You are almost certainly too young to own a car or motorbike, so you will be limited to joining a club you can reach easily by public transport or on a bike. If there are several clubs within easy reach, you should pick the one which appears to encourage its junior members.

A few clubs do not accept members under a certain age. Some allow young players to join, but restrict their use of the facilities to certain hours and certain courts. Sometimes junior members are not allowed to play with seniors. Too many restrictions on your play could affect the progress you make as a player. Ideally you should join a club where there is no limit on the hours you can play, where there is a variety of court surfaces and where you are likely to be 'mixed in' with the more experienced members.

Check whether the club you are interested in joining has a junior tournament and whether it enters a junior team in local league and knock-out competitions.

Word of mouth is the best method of finding a good tennis coach. Ask your friends whether they can recommend a coach.

Setting your sights on a place in the team will give you an incentive to improve your game, and once you are in the team the experience of playing against other clubs will be of great help.

All-weather courts, floodlighting and indoor facilities greatly add to the attraction of a club, allowing members to play at all hours of the day and night and in all weather conditions. However, clubs with these additional facilities usually charge more for membership, or charge extra for their use.

Once you have chosen a club, and been accepted as a member, you will want to make the best use of the facilities. Your tennis club might be the first club you have joined and you would be advised to discover the way a club operates and to learn the rules, if you have not done so before joining.

Most clubs are owned and run by their members. Few tennis clubs are wealthy enough to employ their own staff to do the work of running the club, so many of the jobs that need doing are carried out by the members. You will be a very unpopular member if you only take from the club and never put anything back. Find out if there is anything you can do to help in the running of your club. You will almost certainly have met a member of the club's committee when applying to join and you will be able to enquire from him if there is any way in which you can help.

Most tennis clubs have committees which are elected by the members to run the club. A typical committee will comprise a general secretary who looks after the administration, a membership secretary who deals with the applications of people who want to join, and a financial secretary who looks after money matters. In addition, there is probably someone whose job it is to look after the maintenance of the club house and the grounds, someone who presides over the social functions at the club and someone who deals with junior matters.

By studying the rules, you will be able to discover if there are any special procedures at your club. Most clubs have 'club sessions'. The purpose of these will be to involve new members who might not know anyone else at the club. As you arrive you put your name down on a list, or possibly a peg board, and you will be invited to join in a game at the earliest opportunity. It is because most clubs encourage their members to mix and play with each other, regardless of ability or age, that minimum playing standards are required. Most clubs also have rules limiting the time players can stay on court while other players are waiting. Systems differ from region to region and country to country, but you should become familiar with whatever conventions exist at your club.

Choosing a club with all-weather courts will increase the time you will be able to play. Flood-lighting (*below*) is an attraction offered by some clubs. Before joining a club, check what, if any, restrictions apply to juniors.

As your game improves, you will almost certainly want to enter tournaments. Most tennis clubs have their own junior and senior tournaments for members of the club. Often junior players are allowed to enter the senior event if their playing standard is sufficiently high. If you play tennis at school, your school will probably hold its own annual tournament. But to really test your ability you should enter outside competitions where you will be playing against people you don't meet in the normal course of events. You will be able to find out about such tournaments from your coach or teachers at school, and they might also be able to supply you with entry forms. Otherwise, contact a national or local tennis association.

Most regions have their own tennis championship, although you may have to prove that you have been successful in a club or school competition before your entry is accepted. As a general rule, regional tournaments for young players are divided into age groups, so a player doesn't have to face someone much older than himself. Doing well at regional level will qualify a player to enter a national event—and, of course, success at this level could bring you to the attention of national team selectors.

Never forget that tennis is a game. It was invented for the enjoyment of those who play and for the pleasure it gives those who watch. Get as much enjoyment from playing yourself and try to give pleasure to others.

Success in tennis is like climbing a ladder, with each rung carefully labelled. The top-rung is a singles title at Wimbledon. As a young player you must start at the bottom. Your early ambitions should be to play in your school or club side. You should set your sights on doing well in any tournaments held at school or club level, and when you are feeling confident, enter one of the bigger local events. But remember, when climbing the tennis ladder, take it step by step, stage by stage.

As with most things in life, you will get out of tennis only what you put in. You will have to decide how good you can be and how good you want to be. You will have to decide how big a part of your life you want tennis to become. Climbing to the top of the ladder—playing at Wimbledon, or becoming a professional—will involve tremendous sacrifices on your part, and most probably on the part of your friends and family as well. You may be the sort of person who *has* to be the best at whatever you try, in which case you will not be satisfied with winning a local tournament or being captain of your club side.

But for most people tennis is a way of relaxing in their spare time, a good excuse to get out in the fresh air, a chance to meet other people and an enjoyable way of keeping fit. For them it is enough just to play the game they love, with no thought of glittering trophies or any other rewards beyond the enjoyment of the game.

Index

Acknowledgments

The publishers would like to thank the following organizations and individuals for their kind permission to reproduce the photographs in this book:

All-Sport: (Don Morley) 6–7, 82–83; (Steve Powell) 48 *top*; Barnaby's Picture Library: 34, 59; The Bettman Archives: 74 *bottom*, 76 *top*, 80 *top* and *centre*; Michael R. Carter: 38; Central Press Photos: 79 *top*; Colorsport: 51 *top*; Mary Evans Picture Library: 74 *top*, 75, 77 *top right*, 79 *bottom*; G. Germany: 1, 4–5, 8–32, 36, 39–45, 56, 58, 59 *right*, 60–73, 88–94; Keystone Press Agency Limited: 76 *bottom*, 81 *top*; Le Roye Productions: 35 *top* and *bottom*, 78 *bottom*; Leo Mason: 46–47, 48 *bottom*, 49, 50, 51 *bottom*, 52–55, 84–85; J. Moss: 2–3; Pictor International: Endpapers; Sport and General: 77 *top left*, 80 *bottom*; Sporting Pictures (UK): 81 *bottom*; The Wimbledon Lawn Tennis Museum: 77 *bottom*, 78 *top*.

The author and publisher would also like to thank Kingsley French, Sandy Lutz, David Lacey and David Clark for modelling for the photographs, and the management of the Hotel Los Monteros, Marbella, for providing facilities for the photography.

The diagrams and illustrations in the book were prepared by Astrid Publishing Consultants Ltd.